DIDN'T I FEED YOU YESTERDAY?

Didn't I Feed You Yesterday?

A MOTHER'S GUIDE TO SANITY IN STILETTOS

Laura Bennett

BALLANTINE BOOKS ⌂ NEW YORK

Copyright © 2010 by Laura Bennett

Published in the United States by Ballantine Books, an imprint of The Random House Publishing Group, a division of Random House, Inc., New York.

BALLANTINE BOOKS and colophon are trademarks of Random House, Inc.

ISBN 978-0-345-51637-4

Printed in the United States of America on acid-free paper

www.ballantinebooks.com

987654321

FIRST EDITION

All interior drawings by Robert Best

Book design by Debbie Glasserman

Contents

∎ ∎ ∎ ∎ ∎ ∎ ∎ ∎ ∎ ∎ ∎ ∎

DIDN'T I FEED YOU YESTERDAY?

"Do I really need an owner's manual?"

■

■

■

■

■

■ PREPARE FOR TAKEOFF

NOT LONG AGO I WAS ON AN AIRPLANE WITH ALL six of my children. We were in that purgatory part of the trip between the use of electronic devices and the use of electronic devices. The plane was still being prepared for takeoff, but the area around our seats was already a disaster. Katrina herself couldn't have made such a mess so quickly. The floor was littered with crushed Goldfish and the wrappers from candy bought as appeasement gifts while waiting to board the plane. My husband was in the row behind me with our middle two children, who were engrossed in the age-old argument over the window seat. His row was equally trashed. My two oldest

sat across the aisle from me, all wired up like cyborgs, both of
them gripping their respective iDevices, the sound of music
leaking through headphones momentarily suspended, the
sound of clicking thumbs ditto. They simultaneously looked
over at me with withdrawal and longing, somehow expecting
me to amend the FAA's policy on airwaves.

I noticed over the cacophony that a woman in an ill-
fitting polyester pant suit was standing in the front of the
cabin, making strange hand gestures and trying to tell me
something. I also noticed that she was holding an oxygen
mask. My interest was piqued and her droning words came
into focus.

"When traveling with children, please secure your own
mask before assisting a child." Clearly, this woman was an oracle.

The other passengers seemed to have missed her message,
but it made such clear sense to me: provide yourself with oxygen first, or you will be of no use to your children. If you run
your own life, pursuing your own successes and coping with
your own failures, you won't find yourself dwelling on missed
opportunities or attempting to undo mistakes on the backs of
your kids. Yeah, I thought, if Mama Rose had spent more
time pursuing her own career, wouldn't Gypsy have been able
to keep her clothes on?

The oracle went on to say something like "The nearest
exit might be behind you," which, I have to be honest, didn't
ring as clearly as the oxygen advice, but that was okay, I'd already gotten way more out of this trip than I could have
imagined. I gained a sense of sanity: come what may, if I
chose to do what I needed for myself, rather than trying to
gauge beforehand what my parents, my mate, my friends, or
society expects of me, I would be far more likely to make bet-

ter choices, and to be happier with them. I not only learned that but also got the invaluable advice to remove my Manolos before exiting the plane onto a blow-up ramp. Equally important information if you simply don't want to puncture your life raft, or lose your favorite shoes in the ocean.

Being a mom in the twenty-first century can be a mixed bag of ugly. There are so many opinions about the job you're doing, offered freely and yet at great cost. There are books and blogs and radio programs and mom groups and lactation consultants and magazines and on and on. Never has there been so much accessible and contradictory information floating in the ether of parenting, and never has the concept of "my way or the highway" been so brutally administered. We have collectively micromanaged our pregnancies and written our superfluous Birth Plans and succumbed to the pressure of feeding our kids 100 percent organic hand-milled baby food using a reduced carbon footprint. These unrealistic goals have created a population of neurotic mothers whose neurotic kids inevitably end up at my house on a playdate.

I have chosen a more retro approach to parenting. For one thing, I have six children, a very old-fashioned number. And by having so many I have discovered one of the great secrets to being a perfect mother: *there is no such thing.*

From the day my mother picked up her first Dr. Spock guide to the onslaught of the *How to Expect What Your Baby Expects of You* types of titles, there have been scores of books on every facet of the parenting equation. When I was first pregnant, twenty years ago, times were different. There were no Internet chat rooms or message boards where women felt free to demoralize other mothers. But with each child I've produced, there has come an increasing tide of perfectionism that has slowly overtaken basic human instinct. Don't get me wrong; I like a healthy, well-adjusted child as much as the next person. But do I really need an owner's manual? Don't you just turn it on and fix it when it's broken?

Call me crazy, but it seems to me that the spike in postpartum depression has occurred hand in hand with the increase of parenting advice available to new moms. The plummet of hormones and the uptick of expectations cross over each other in the most fragile of environments—a healing mother and a helpless, squalling bundle of nerves. Childbirth sucks, and it's frankly a miracle that we're not all dead from it—it's no wonder some women walk away with invisible scars to go with the visible ones. But childbirth is a cakewalk compared to motherhood. The women I know who keep focused on their own survival typically break through the web of high-strung mothering that has unfortunately become the norm. Why on earth would a complete stranger ever ask you whether you breastfed or not? I might be a throwback, but I think who sucks on me and how often in the privacy of my own home is my business.

I have consistently put my neck on the chopping block, both as a mother and as a woman—most famously during a stint on a reality show called *Project Runway,* where people compete to be the next top fashion designer. I had zero related experience when I auditioned for the show, but I loved watching it so much I thought, Why not me? I got myself in the room, and went further than I could have ever imagined. Through my actions, I showed my kids what was possible, and though they may have gone unbathed those few weeks I was away, I assure you they survived.

I am frequently asked, How can you possibly manage six children? And work? And look so put together? When pressed, I will admit that my approach is twofold: I always take care of myself, and I parent my children my way, not the way others expect me to. I get my oxygen first. When I stop and think about it, I often find that my worst days are in direct proportion to how far I let myself drift away from that yellow plastic mask. Motherhood is the hardest job in the world. Around kid number four I realized that the only way to survive it is to have a sense of humor. After all, the tragic often becomes comedic in the retelling.

"You just had to buy a new baby, didn't you?"

■

■

■

■

■

■ FAMILY PORTRAIT

IF BY MODERN-DAY STANDARDS I HAVE A LOT OF CHIL-
dren, then by New York City standards I have single-handedly
created a population explosion and ruined any chance for
other families to attend private school due to my abuse of the
sibling preference policy. A family of eight in Manhattan is
practically grounds for forcible commitment to Bellevue.
How could we be so crazy?

To me, having six children is completely normal. I don't
really get couples who choose to stop at one or two. That's like
going to Vegas and only playing one hand of blackjack, or

throwing the dice twice. My curiosity gets the best of me: I want to see what genetic cocktail Lady Luck has to offer.

As if I needed another reason, every package of eight-pound baby comes with a special toy surprise—a designer handbag, an art deco bracelet, or a pair of fabulous shoes. My husband's gifts are incentive enough to endure nine months of pregnancy. And I look at each occasion as my last chance. Once we get a new baby home and are faced with the added expense, I figure there will be no more gifts.

Having so many children was hardly a conscious decision, not something I set out to accomplish, but it has taken the pressure off all of the concerned parties. I don't have to be so meticulous about every little thing. If I lose one somewhere, there are extras. We have an heir, a spare, another spare, and three more spares. I'm not really sure how that happened. Of course I know, technically, *how* it happened, and I admit I didn't do anything to stop it. Sometimes it was a matter of "Oh, look, honey, the baby is walking! He has grown so fast. Time to have another!" Those were the planned ones. Then there was the time my husband, Peter, came to me with a urine-laden plastic stick emblazoned with a magenta plus sign and asked, "Is this yours?" I replied, "I'm pretty sure it's yours." That was a surprise one.

Planned or not, however each one came about, on most days I am happy to have them. And so I find myself with six dependent souls and the responsibility of getting them safely from infancy to adulthood with minimal mental damage to them or me. Of course if one of them gets into drugs, or we run into the occasional disability, it's no big deal. I don't have all my eggs in one perfect little basket; I don't need every child to be a straight-A, Ivy League–admitted music-and-sports prodigy. I have the luxury of accepting each of them as they are, quirks, disabilities, genetic mutations, and all.

CLEO

"Where did you get that?" I asked, waking from a nap to a familiar smell.

"I called Domino's," my daughter answered with a shrug.

"Where did you get the money?" I probed, groggy and bewildered.

"The bottom of your purse."

"Did you tip?"

"Twenty percent." She winked, radiant with pride. "I got your favorite."

Cleo was five years old. We'd been watching something on the television and I had dozed off, overwhelmed with fatigue-induced narcolepsy. It was a common occurrence for me in those days. I had been living in Texas and I wanted out of my marriage, so I formulated an escape plan based on higher education. When I was accepted to the graduate program for architecture at Columbia University in New York City, I took my daughter, left my husband, and moved north and east, suddenly becoming a broke, single working mother and full-time student. Cleo had spent the first four years of her life in a booster seat under my drafting table at the University of Houston; she would spend the next few lean, exhausting years in the first character-building situation of her life. And build character she did. There were days when we had to walk to school across Central Park because we didn't have $1.50 to take the bus, but being penniless and raising a kid by myself never felt like obstacles. I was living in Disneyland for grown-ups, swinging from chandeliers with Cleo right beside me, fixture for fixture. Of course there were times when she was the adult, a doppelgänger of Tatum

O'Neal in *Paper Moon* right down to her little banged hair-cut.

"Get up, Mom, you'll be late for work," she would prod.

"You're not going out with that loser again, are you?" she would accurately judge.

"You are not leaving the house in *that* dress," she would scold. I barely had time to parent—much less overparent—but, thanks in good part to my abject neglect, Cleo has grown into an independent, self-sufficient, and fearless adult.

When Cleo was nine, she announced at Thanksgiving that she was a vegetarian and would no longer be eating anything with a face. This is not that unusual, particularly among girls who love animals as fiercely as Cleo does. The only thing I take issue with is her choice of terminology. If she wants to be accurate, she should call herself a "pastatarian" or a "Cheeriotarian," as I cannot recall an actual vegetable ever clearing her front teeth. Corn on the cob and French fries don't count, in my opinion; they are starches, devoid of nutrients other than the dirt or the occasional corn worm that evades detection. If you ask her brother Truman to describe his sister, he will say, "She has big boobs and only eats cereal."

When I met Peter, he instantly understood that Cleo and I were a package deal. Things moved quickly; we married, and in three years we had two more children. With the body count steadily growing, Cleo decided it was time to strike out on her own—she wanted to go to boarding school. It's possible that she was too embarrassed by the repetitive proof of her parents having sex, and needed to get out of town, but I think the reason was more likely her insane love of horses. What horses do for girls is buy time, giving them a few extra years before they must discover boys. I do mean the "buying time" part literally, because those years don't come cheap. Ever industrious, Cleo helped by mucking out the neighbor's barn upstate in exchange for riding lessons. I was not at all surprised when she started on her own to research boarding schools that offered riding as a centerpiece of the curriculum, and more than a little relieved that we wouldn't have to go through the grueling school application process in Manhattan. Being her usual assertive self, she compiled a list of options and set up appointments for the three of us to visit. She also filled out all the applications and wrote the necessary essays completely on her own. Talk about low maintenance. In the end she chose Foxcroft, a beautiful all-girl high school in Virginia, and achieved her double goal of riding every day and wearing pajamas to class.

Many friends and family attended Cleo's graduation, but I couldn't be there, sequestered as I was for *Project Runway.* She wore a long white gown that I sewed for her. As I toiled in the workroom at Parsons, a captive of reality programming, I occasionally had enough mental acuity to think about Cleo. I realized that sending her off to boarding school was the greatest sacrifice I had ever made in my life. The moments I missed with her—watching her dress for a date or celebrate after a victory on the hockey field—are lost to me. She thrived, grew, cultivated friendships, and gained worldviews that have formed her life, and I was not a part of the process. It would have been selfish to keep her from leaving when she was clearly so ready, but it was nearly unbearable to let her go.

PEIK

"You should get a job at Hooters," Peik once told his big sister.

"You should get a job as Dad," she shot back.

I hope I made the right choice to marry Peter and bear his spawn, because when I gave birth to Peik I suddenly had two of him. This would be the natural place to make a Pete and re-Pete joke, but I will spare you. Apart from his hair color, Peik is in every way—physical, emotional, habitual—a clone of his father. I know what you're thinking: what kind of name is Peik? My husband once had a girlfriend whose brother was named Peik, and Peter loved the name more than the girl-friend, apparently. Some women would be offended by this connection to a husband's past love life, but not me. I have no problem with the source of the name; what I do have a prob-lem with is the name itself. Is it for a boy or a girl? How do I pronounce it? Does it involve that obnoxious "i before e" rule? I fear I have given my son a long and frustrating way of introducing himself to strangers.

"Hi, I'm Peik."

"Come again?"

"Peik. As in 'bake,' or 'shake.'"

"Pike?"

"No, PAKE, rhymes with RAKE."

"What kind of name is Pack?"

"It's either high Scandinavian or low German, depending on the Google search return. Though my dad contends it's Dutch for Peter. And it's PAKE, not Pack."

"Nice to meet you, Peck."

Luckily, Peik's sense of humor is very dry and advanced beyond his years, no doubt because he was weaned on Monty Python. As a very small child, he would push a toy grocery cart around the apartment, calling "Bring out your dead!" in a lame British accent. Since his sister is seven years older than he, his early exposure to *The Simpsons* and then *Family Guy* might only have increased his odds of getting thrown into pre-k detention for trying to be the funny kid. I know it's in vogue to obsess over a child's "screen time," but movies and television have helped develop and shape his sense of humor, and I personally find him very entertaining. And honestly, isn't that ultimately what children are for? To entertain their parents? Not in an ex-child-star-turned-to-drugs kind of way, more like a shooting-at-their-feet-to-make-them-dance sort of thing.

Peik's movements are lethargic even though his mind spins at warp speed. Always three mental steps ahead, by the time he enters a room he has assessed what will be asked of him and has already found a way out of doing it, usually by slipping off to his bedroom to mousterbate at his computer until food is served. I call this "the thinking man's lazy." I suspect he spends that room time Googling "how to torture younger siblings," as he is definitely the family rabble-rouser. On the rare occasion when the house is at peace and all the other children are engaged in quiet activity, Peik will let out a rebel yell and run through the house with his pants around his ankles, distributing wedgies. This is the only time he moves his feet unasked. He also has an uncanny ability to push people's buttons. Back when he was six, he taped fourteen-year-old Cleo's zebra-striped bra and panties to the front door of our apartment building. In the middle of Manhattan. When she came home with a couple of friends she was so horrified she didn't speak to Peik for—well, come to think of it, she still hasn't spoken to him.

Sibling panty raids aside, I never would have pegged Peik to be a player by the tender age of thirteen. He comes from two long lines of late bloomers. I was too busy drawing or sewing to notice that there were boys in the room until I was seventeen, and the fact that I resembled Olive Oyl, complete with the disproportionally big feet, kept even the most desperate boys at bay. When I found Peter hiding behind a dusty piece of bachelor furniture, he was fifty years old and had never been married, the ultimate slow starter.

Of all the boys in the house, I'm not sure how Peik became the stud, enjoying his choice of available girls. If my six-year-old, Pierson, started chatting online with girls and setting up dates tomorrow I wouldn't be surprised: at four years old, he announced, "My face is my fortune," and carefully began choosing his school wardrobe. But Peik was a shy and apprehensive boy who refused to leave the safety of his stroller at the park. When he started pre-kindergarten, I had to sit in the school library every day well into January because he would cry if he realized I wasn't on the premises. So how did he come to be the one roaming New York City streets with a girl on his arm? It can't be his mastery of poetic language—Peik's computer sits next to mine, so I have seen exactly how he lures in the next babe.

> Peik: movee?
>
> Girl: k
>
> Peik: sat?
>
> Girl: k
>
> Peik: lol c u

No, it is certainly not his flowery prose that is charming the girls. Probably not his academic standing, either. While he is perfectly willing to study during school, his workday ends when the bell rings—an apathy reflected in his grades. Athletic prowess? Not so much—Peik's the pasty-colored one with slumpy posture in the black skinny jeans, his fingers calloused from playing guitar. His handsome face? Yes, but only once he grows into those huge teeth and gets that hair out of his eyes. He does have a killer sense of humor, but I can't imagine any teenaged girl finding wedgies or repeated "Death of Kenny" reenactments hilarious. Though Lord knows I think he's wildly entertaining, so maybe a girl or two are on to something.

It's not that I worry that anything untoward might happen. Manhattan is a great place to raise teens. This may seem like the big bad city, but it's hard for kids to get into too much trouble here. They travel in packs, tend to hang out in public places, and, best of all, don't drive. Believe me, Peik would much rather be in the suburbs where kids can have sex on the trampoline in the backyard after school.

I realize I'm showing all the signs of a mother lamenting the inevitable independence of her child, grieving the needy toddler so reliant on her. But I swear, I'm not. I have six children; I've been through this before with no problem. My daughter is twenty and has been away at college for three years now. There are four more boys after Peik, so I still have plenty of preschool graduations, holiday singalongs, and field trips to the circus coming my way. If you see me misty-eyed at a promotion ceremony from kindergarten to first grade, it's probably only because I couldn't defer my appearance.

When Peik was a small boy, he paid very little attention to me. His first word was "Cleo," followed quickly by "Daddy," and I would have to say that that is exactly the place and order of his loyalties, as much as he may love to torture his sister. I sometimes feel that, if he could have said them, "Hey, lady" would have been his next words. Now that he is a teenager, the distance between us is slowly and unexpectedly closing, taking me by sentimental surprise. I'm just starting to get to know the boy, so maybe that's why I'm not so ready for him to be a man. Lately he has become more affectionate toward me, and often now takes my hand when we are walking down the street. The hand is still usually filthy, but I'm honored to hold it for as long as he will offer, calluses, warts, or infectious hand-borne diseases be damned.

TRUMAN

As mentioned, my husband was fifty and had never been married when I met him, having had a series of long-term relationships that cracked apart at the mere mention of betrothal. It should have been no surprise to me, then, that when it came to naming children post-Peik, Peter would show signs of commitment anxiety. It seems his other exes didn't have interesting enough brothers to continue what would clearly be seen as a pathological course of action. Our second son bore the brunt of this indecision, to the extent that the hospital warned us not to leave the premises until that child had a name. I called their bluff, and told them that if my insurance company wanted to foot the bill until my husband decided on a name, I would be more than happy to stay. Peter overthinks everything, so I knew it could be awhile. Typically, the hospital registers vital details with the government agencies that send you convenient little things like birth certificates and social security cards, but if you leave without naming a child, you are solely responsible. Had the administrative staff instead said to me, "You're going to have to name him Red Tape if you don't name him right now," I might have understood the severity of the situation. Instead, though, we blithely left the hospital and proceeded to call the baby "the baby" for the next three months. He was finally named at a cocktail party by some of my oldest and drunkest friends. "Truman," they chorused after a good deal of slurred deliberation. Hmm, I pondered: flaming gay New York prize-winning writer and socialite, or daring bomb-dropping presidential warrior? Not a bad range of options. "Truman" stuck fast, but it was many, many years before I screwed up the courage to face the bureaucrats and officially have his name changed from "Baby White Male."

Of all my children, Truman shows me the most affection, and has valiantly lived up to his honest and stalwart name. Perhaps because he breast-fed until he was four years old, he has developed a disturbing fondness for skin-to-skin contact. At nine years old, he still throws himself at me for a hug and kiss when he gets home from school—did he just cop a feel? I would take his mother love as a compliment if he didn't show most people the same level of affection. When he was five, we took him to see Momix at the Joyce Theater, an establishment known for its dedication to modern dance and the avant-garde. It was a beautiful performance, at the end of which the dancers left the stage and exited through the audience, waving to the crowd jubilantly on both sides. Truman, his small freckled face streaked with joyful tears, leaped to his feet and stopped one dancer in mid stride by embracing her tightly around the waist. I was simultaneously proud and jealous. But then I worried that someday this polymorphous perversity might be misconstrued as sexual predation, his face was so firmly pressed against her breasts. I have also noticed that he simply cannot pass the baby without unsnapping Finn's onesie (if he's wearing one, which he typically isn't), stroking that soft belly, and saying "Good baby, nice baby." It's sweet. But kind of creepy.

Truman is also our natural athlete; he can play catch with small children endlessly, delighting in their every move. And he is our greatest hope for higher education, because he fences. This sport is so obscure that it is actually possible to become nationally ranked, something that would never happen in basketball or baseball. Being nationally ranked in anything looks impressive on an application, and it's surprising how many colleges have fencing teams. Of course, what I pay for lessons will never equal what he might receive in scholarship money, but if he is going to have an extracurricular activity it may as well be one that is going to give us a glimmer of breaking even. He works hard at school and always has a new and interesting dance routine. His best attribute though, is his red hair. He gets that from his dad, who is now famous for his Einstein shock of white hair but once was russet-locked. *My* red hair comes from a box at the drugstore, because I'm worth it. But because I have a ginger boy, only "Hi, My Name Is Rhonda" knows for sure.

PIERSON

When Baby White Male turned three, another boy was born, as if I needed another boy. Until I had Pierson, it seemed as though I was merely a genetically recessive host womb, designed to produce a child in your image. Naming this one took less time than naming Truman, but it was still a dithering affair. I suggested, as I had twice before, Peter, thinking it the quickest way to please my husband and get us out of paperwork jail. He was having none of that, but did agree to a derivation, and so we came up with Pierson: "Peter's son," in some decrepit foreign language. It was enough to buy our release from the hospital, and seemed like an entirely appropriate moniker, but eventually we realized he looks exactly like me.

Pierson prides himself on being "sexy." He is six and it is his favorite word. He uses it to describe himself, but also cars, skateboards, dances, food, girls, and shoes—anything at all.

Our family has grown accustomed to his constant use of the word, but it tends to throw off strangers.

"Did he just say *sexy*?"

Pierson works his sexy image: he always makes sure he has his gorgeous curly brown hair styled with product, and he's been choosing his own clothes since he was born: screaming when I would hazard to diaper him with Barney instead of Elmo. He did have a point. Lately, his carefully cultivated look requires an abundance of flames and skulls: his signature motifs.

"Mom, today I am Emo."

"I thought you were Goth."

"That was this morning."

"What happened to yesterday's Sk8r boy? I was kinda getting the hang of him."

"Oh, he'll be back, don't worry. Would you like to see my show?"

After painstakingly creating a new look, he will pull two Nelson benches together to form a catwalk, and give us his best runway strut. When he receives a compliment on his leather motorcycle jacket, he responds with a wink of his mischievous light green eyes. If Truman is voted most likely to be a sexual predator, Pierson would be voted most likely to be gay—and that is fine with me, because God knows I could use another feminine force in this house.

Pierson loves to shop and hates to bathe, eat, or sleep. When I hear new parents talk about how the baby doesn't sleep through the night, I have to strangle the bitter laugh that would reveal the doom I've faced with this child. I am such a light sleeper that I practically lie awake waiting to be awakened by him, eager to show me which outfit he plans to wear to school.

One of Pierson's proud distinguishing factors is that the second and third toes on both his feet are connected, sort of webbed halfway up. I guess when you are one of so many siblings anything that sets you apart is something to embrace, even if it is a mild genetic mutation. Normally, I would find an attribute like this disturbing, like the human version of a six-toed cat, but I have to admit that on this handsome child, it is kind of sexy.

LARSON

In a "What were you thinking?" move, a year and a half after Pierson, Larson was born. Exhausted from caring for the four previous children, and clean out of ideas, we took the easy way out and went with "Laura's son." Naturally, he looks exactly like Peter. Now I have three of him.

"Hey, Lawa, can you get me some owpol jus?"

"Sure, and you can call me Mom."

Larson is an outrageously outgoing little four-year-old, whose relentless friendliness drives him to strike up conversations with everybody. However, because of developmental speech problems, his conversations tend to be a garbled stream of excited rhetoric, generally responded to with "What?" or a confused smile. When he was less than two, Larson's adenoids were enlarged and infected, and his ears filled with a viscous fluid as a result of a series of undetected ear infections. He clearly has a very high pain threshold: he rarely peeped about anything hurting him. Apparently, if you can't hear very well, speaking can be tricky. Once he had surgery to remove the residual junk from the infections and started speech therapy he quickly made great progress, though the exact extent of his disabilities has never been clear.

This doesn't seem to bother him in any way. Larson spends his cheerful days surfing YouTube with the alacrity of a teenage boy and obsessively changing from superhero costume to superhero costume while begging for NRFB MIB *Blue's Clues* items he finds on eBay.

Because Larson has been designated a child with "special needs," he has an entourage—an ear, nose, and throat specialist, a pediatric prosthodontist, occupational therapists, speech therapists, and play therapists. It is a supporting cast with Larson as the shining star. We have also learned that when you can't breathe through your nose because your adenoids are enlarged, you breathe through your mouth, and your tooth enamel pays the price. We had Larson's decaying little front teeth capped, and ten minutes later he knocked one out by accident. With his ear-to-ear smile and one large center tooth he is very much the perfect, living comic strip character. The Larsonator.

For a while we weren't sure what was "wrong" with Larson—as in, why he didn't seem to progress the way the other children had. Yes, there was the physical problem, but there was also a time when we didn't know if that was all there was to it. He had a too-happy, goofy quality about him. Autism was ultimately ruled out because of his intense desire to communicate. He went through quite a few tests, including one for intelligence quotient. The administrator asked Larson to point to the butterfly picture in a book. He responded by getting up and performing an entire dance. He started by squirming on the floor like a caterpillar, and then rolled up in a blanket, unrolling from the blanket, opening his wings, and then flying off, fluttering around the room with a large grin on his face. The tester looked at me—I swear she had tears in her eyes—and gently told me that because he did not point to the two-dimensional drawing he had failed the question. I blinked. She blinked. Larson fluttered some more. I looked at him and held my tongue. We all knew in that moment that he was going to be fine, whether the test results indicated intelligence or not. At first, I felt angry that the test had to be so rigid, but I couldn't blame the administrator. She saw what I saw. In the next moment I felt incredibly grateful, knowing all the difficulties that mothers go through to help their children survive far worse than a delay in speech. If this is all I get, I thought, then I'll take it and run for the hills.

All of my children have inherited some degree of artistic ability, but Larson's is different. His brain had adapted to the speech problem by rapidly increasing his skills with pencil and paper. Even when he was as young as two, he would watch a show on TV and then go and draw everything he saw. In detail. Okay, I thought, he's my Rain Man. We knew there was something bright in there, it just had some trouble getting out, and his more unusual quirks, such as insisting he wear his pants backward, every single day, or the fact that a tiny loose thread would drive him so nuts he would eventually cut up the entire garment, gave us pause. Larson was always very talkative, but his baby babble developed into a language of his own. Now that he's had a year of intensive speech therapy, we know what he was trying to say, and it goes something like this:

"Lawa, Twuman isn't pwaying by da ruwes, and Piewson hit da baby, and in da udder woom Peik is pwaying wid da mouse agin and you debinetly tole him not to. Oh, and Petew cawed to say he'd be wate fow dinnew."

In other words, he's a tattletale. He's constantly commenting on the injustices and broken rules around him, not because he expects us to do anything about it, but just to let us know he's watching every last one of us.

FINN

And finally, there is Finn, which stands for Finis, Finito, Finished. We got Pierson and Larson's names wrong; I really really hope we got this one right. As he is still so young, I haven't been able to peg his personality, but he seems to be a happy boy—very rough-and-tumble—and he never shies from the action. If his brothers are wrestling, he will climb right to the top of the pile. If they are on our homemade stage, rocking out, Finn will grab the closest thing to a guitar he can find—a piece of pizza, for instance—and join in the jam. Finn will find his way to the middle of everything, from a dance contest to a fencing bout.

Although he is beloved by his brothers, this boy is no angel, which is probably why he fits in so well. I was sitting at my desk working on an article when I heard a series of dull thuds coming from the kitchen. I decided I had better go investigate, and sure enough I found Finn up to his usual trouble. He was standing in front of the fridge in his diaper with a dozen eggs, dropping them to the floor one by one like a B-52 bomber.

"Why eggs?" I asked as he got ready to lob another. The look on his face was pure satisfaction.

"Look at this mess, Mom!" Pierson scolded when he entered the kitchen to check out why I was going postal. "You just *had* to buy a new baby, didn't you? Now he's bad and we are all stuck with him."

We still call Finn the baby, and probably always will,

though at almost two years old, he is starting to talk. He's also my only blondie, with a tuft of curly hair that makes me want to card it and knit a tiny sweater. Finn is my celebrity baby. As my pregnancy became increasingly obvious during *Project Runway*, much of the chatter surrounding the show focused squarely on my giant belly, and viewers got a kick out of watching me sew myself into larger and larger glam wear. When he was born, *People* magazine did a two-page spread on him. In fact, when we were still in the hospital watching CNN, his little name ran across the ticker! Even Peter, notoriously hard to impress, was thrilled. Apparently, by nerd standards the crawl is the ultimate sign that you have arrived. Now that I think of it, my contestant agreement for *Project Runway* was so intrusive, the network may actually own him. I should probably be receiving child support from the producers.

I HAVE A FAVORITE CHILD. I HEAR YOU GASPING IN HORROR. I ACTU-ally believe every mother does, but won't admit it. It's the dirty little secret of motherhood. Why is it so horrible? It's not *Sophie's Choice* or anything. I'm not saying I don't love all of my children equally, just that I don't always like all of them, at least not every day (or week, or month, or year).

I have favorite shoes, movies, and foods; why not a favorite child? It's not as though I won't help you with your homework if you're not my favorite. The task is just less insufferable for me with some of my children than with others. My children know I play favorites; they actually compete to be held in my highest esteem. We call their rank order the List.

"Don't do that," I say, "you'll go to the bottom of the List."

"If I rub your feet, will I go to the top of the List?" Truman says, willing to work for it.

"Just put me at the top," says Peik, angling for a freebie.

"Mom, I'm paying my own way through college," Cleo helpfully points out. "I'm working two jobs and saving my education fund to start up a business when I graduate." There is a pause. "Where am I on the List?"

"I sure do love you," Pierson says, applying himself to me like spray tan. "There isn't a List, is there, it's just me, right?"

"Lawa, Pake is twying to gib me a wedgie," Larson says, not really understanding what's going on, but smart enough to take his brother down a peg.

"Gaga baga dada mama ist," Finn squeaks.

I prefer certain childhood stages to others, and by virtue of being in one of the preferred stages, a child can find itself higher on the List. I find babies cute and innocent, while teenagers seem hell bent on ruining my life; I'll forgive a ruined dozen of eggs more quickly than a lost-for-the-fifth-time cell phone.

Some of my kids operate like me, so I understand them better. These are the ones who, less intellectually gifted, work harder to succeed. Some of my children are better suited to my husband's personality: he totally gets them, while I stand there dumbfounded. I find nothing more frustrating than a child who is superintelligent but uses that intelligence to find ways to beat the system.

If you swear you have no favorite, and think you are fooling your kids, you're wrong. Kids are short; they aren't stupid. I find that, just as personalities are formed partly by birth order, they are also formed by preference order. I know a woman who thought her brother's name was MySonPaul, she was so clearly not her mother's favorite. Today this woman is a successful publishing executive, driven by her childhood striving to be on top. Her brother still lives at home.

Not only am I convinced that this competition is healthy, but I would also venture to say that overprotective mothering does more damage. So bring me that List, and who wants to give me a back rub?

I've given up hoping for another girl, and have really gotten the swing of a houseful of men. But don't think even for a minute that I don't wonder what would happen if we were to go bananas and throw the dice again. People say I'm crazy when I tell them I'm open to just one more. Really—six, seven, eight, what's the difference? Peter and I are already grossly outnumbered. We have no current plans to have any more children, but if we did get Finn's name wrong, we would just throw another kid on the pile with the rest of them and it would be as well loved, exquisitely neglected, and—we hope—entertaining as all the others.

"I can see trapping a man with one
pregnancy, but five?"

MANIFEST DESTINY

LATELY, PETER IS SHOWING A DISTURBING INTER-est in card tricks. He learns them from videos on YouTube.

"Come see this, kids," he says as he tries to get the five boys to gather around. After the first chorus of "How'd you do that?" and "Do that again!" they typically lose interest and move back to their video games, TV shows, and guitars.

"Peter," I say to him in an indignant tone.

"What?" he replies, all innocent.

"What? *What?* Card tricks? What the hell are you thinking? Do you know what this means?" I almost shout. "Who does card tricks, Peter? Think! Old men! That's who does card tricks. This officially makes you an old man!"

While I can take some solace in the fact that he learns these tricks on the Internet, a venue not normally associated with the oxygen tank crowd, the truth is that performing card tricks is second only to writing letters of complaint and carrying an AARP card as a true indicator that you have officially arrived at old age. It is not that I mind if Peter is old. I actually like being married to an older man; it makes me feel young by comparison, and it means that no matter how old I get I'll always be a babe to him. It is true that at least his letters of complaint are usually about the inefficiency of an interface or a flaw in the calculation system of a financial website, but card tricks still cross the line.

It seems like a lifetime ago. I was living in Houston, and one of my girlfriends came to visit. Kathryn and I had worked together folding panties at Victoria's Secret, but then her husband was transferred and they had moved to Kansas City.

"Let's go get our fortunes told," she said, telling me about this guy in Houston she had heard of who was reported to be the real thing. I demurred for myself—I don't need a roadmap to navigate my life—but agreed to drive Kathryn to an address an hour across town, not such an unusual distance in the urban sprawl of Texas. We arrived at a typical-looking apartment complex with no discernible universe-shaking auras, located the proper apartment, and were shown into what could have passed for any retiree condo south of the Mason-Dixon Line. No red velvet curtains with thick gold fringe, no crystal balls, not even a single neon sign flashing promises of the future being unlocked. Nope, just beige décor and an equally beige-looking guy in his late thirties. After awkward hellos, he showed me to a beige couch while he and Kathryn retreated to a breakfast nook table graced with nothing more supernatural than a deck of tarot cards, the one and only indication that spirits were about to descend on suburbia.

Sensing a presence nearby, I found nestled next to me against a beige pillow a tiny, ancient, beige Chihuahua. She moved a little, arthritically, and waggled what looked like long, stringy moles hanging from her grayed jowls. The psychic lovingly introduced us, and I felt that though this guy was probably a fraud, he must at least be a good person to care for such an unfortunate little creature.

Kathryn's reading began with a gathering and a shuffling of the deck. I didn't really pay much attention to the peek into Kathryn's future, as Hanging-Mole Dog transfixed me. I didn't mind sharing the sofa with it, but I was definitely trying to avoid physical contact. I was interrupted from my task when the psychic cleared his throat. I looked up and saw him staring at me.

"I see you in the future in upstate New York or Connecticut with a man who has blue eyes, white hair, and a mustache," he offered me from the cosmos. "Living in a raised ranch house." He stopped talking. Apparently that was all the great otherworld had for me.

"Wow, okay, thanks," I said. He then turned his attention back to Kathryn. I grew up in the South and had lived there all my life. At that moment, I certainly had no plans, immediate or otherwise, to move to the Northeast. I hadn't even heard of a "raised" ranch house before; it's not something they condone in architecture school, and it didn't sound like a future home to be excited about. In fact, I had heard "raised ranch" as "razed" ranch, as in "no longer standing," or "bulldozed," or even worse, "demolished by an ugly-house-hating tornado."

My father has blue eyes, white hair, and a mustache, so I assumed there was some kind of weird Electra mixed signal being sent. I was married to a man with dark hair, dark eyes, and no mustache, and he wouldn't have been thrilled about the outside chance that any of this revelation might be true. I filed it under "Never mind" and eventually put the whole episode behind me.

Four years later, I was living in the Northeast. A new acquaintance invited me to her house for a dinner party. These were my freewheeling newly single days—wine, roses, dinner parties, dates with lots of eligible bachelors, quiet nights at home with pizza and Cleo. Sure, I said, I'd love to. I'm always up for meeting a new roomful of people. I'm like a human party favor—throw me into a group of unknowns and I'll have met everyone by the end of the evening. I put on my discount Donna Karan, strapped on some sexy heels, and made my way to an address down in SoHo. Outside the building I noticed a man just standing there, looking up at the parapets, looking down at the sidewalk, then pacing back and forth.

"Excuse me," I said, eyeing him for a bit and deciding he looked the type, "are you here for the party?" He nodded. "Would you like to ride up with me?" He smiled and said yes. We chatted in the elevator; we chatted in the foyer; we chatted during drinks before dinner; we chatted until we were seated. He was easy to converse with. He was also an architect, but we didn't discuss architecture, which was a huge relief because "What's your favorite building in New York?" between architects is as tired as "What's your sign?" for the rest of the trolling population. When dinner was called and we all gathered around the table, I saw his tiny place card off down the table, next to what looked to be another single woman; the company around me soon carried me away into other possibilities. I was popular in the room that night, and I lost sight of my pre-dinner friend until it was time to leave. As the other guests were saying their goodbyes to our hostess I sought him out to share a cab uptown.

The next day I was in my office when a Peter Shelton called. The name didn't ring any bells.

"Hi, this is Peter," he said. "We met last night. I'm doing a modified bed check."

"A bed check?"

"Yes, I'm calling to see if you took Mr. Deep Pockets up on his offer to go to the Cowgirl Hall of Fame gala in Fort Worth."

"Oh, please," I huffed, as though I had never had any intention of going on this jaunt. I was a bit surprised that Peter had overheard that particular tidbit. The truth was, in my newly single dating days I was up for anything; but I had a set of architectural drawings to get out of the office, and Mr. Pockets's private jet was leaving soon. I glanced at the clock. No dice. I was about to cut my losses and engage Mr. Shelton in some date-driven witty banter when the phone went dead. My office was being wired for a new computer system, and a guy with a tool belt poked his head in my door and said, "Oops." I looked at the phone in my hand and mused over Peter's choice of the term "bed check." When I had first moved to New York and left my first husband back in Texas he would brokenheartedly call at all hours, an activity my close friends and I began referring to as "bed checks." I placed the phone back in the cradle and looked at the clock to see if maybe I could still swing liftoff.

Three days later, my friend Julie offered to take Cleo to a movie. Free babysitting for a single mother is not an opportunity to miss. I phoned the hostess from the dinner party to get

Peter's number, and without regard for the Rules I bravely dialed it.

"Would you like to go for a drink tonight?"

"How about tomorrow? I have to work late."

"No, it has to be tonight. What time are you done?"

"Ten?"

"Perfect."

Julie took Cleo to the movies and Peter and I went to a bar near my apartment for martinis. I wore the dress and shoes from the night of the dinner party—it was my best outfit, and honestly, the man didn't notice. Probably because he still wears the same clothes he wore in boarding school, nametags intact, but also because he just doesn't get hung up on superficial details. Owing, no doubt, to the martinis, I don't really remember much from that first date, except Peter sitting in the gutter trying to tie the tiny ankle strap of my high-heeled shoe.

Then, breaking every other rule in the dating book, he ignored both my drunkenness and my high-maintenance footwear and called the very next morning to invite me for the weekend to his house upstate. With my child. Who does that? Let's see, I thought. Fifty years old, never married, no children. Two possible explanations: severe commitment phobia or gay. What did I have to lose? I certainly wasn't ready for a second husband, and really, what single mom doesn't need all the gay help she can get?

I drove. There were two things I had kept from my marriage: my daughter and my Porsche 911 (a girl's got to have a sexy getaway car). I was going broke paying for a garage in New York City, so this was my big chance to show off the Porsche. The weekend found us speeding up the Palisades Parkway, headed to Peter's house in Cold Spring, New York.

"So what kind of a house is it?" I asked, curious about what style a fellow architect might have chosen.

"Nothing fancy." He sounded slightly embarrassed. "Just a raised ranch."

I immediately turned the wheel to the side of the road and threw on the brakes. I got out of the car, walked around to Peter, leaned down, and looked in at him. Blue eyes. Mustache. White hair. I looked up at the side of the road and saw the "Welcome to New York" sign. Peter and Cleo both just stared at me. Raised. Flicking. Ranch. The entire beige-infused psychic episode came flooding back to me with amazing clarity.

"You are my destiny," I told him. I didn't stop to think about how a fifty-year-old bachelor would take such a revelation. It just popped out. Peter continued to sit there. He didn't get out of my car and run away down the Palisades. I returned to my side of the car and drove off (into the sunset). We have never looked back.

PETER'S MOTHER TOLD ME THAT HE WAS GAY. I GUESS THAT'S WHAT A mother tells herself after watching fifty years of her son's failed relationships. Or she could have seen the destiny on the wall and was looking to scare me off. The reason might have been the location of our first Big Date: Africa, a marked upgrade from Peter's usual helicopter ride over Manhattan. Or perhaps what troubled her was the fact that we didn't bother to get married before we had Peik. Anyway, something about me threw her, and all the other people in Peter's life, way off. They came just short of telling me I "trapped" him by getting pregnant. After all, a determined bachelor who had slunk away from three engagements—once, after the invitations had gone out—*must have been* tricked by a pretty determined hussy. I can see trapping a man with one pregnancy, but five? The man is obviously a willing participant. Even so, one of Peter's past loves still describes him as the love of her life. Others continue to call and write or stop by his office to catch up with him. I get the feeling they all see him as the one that got away, and I'm pretty sure they're on to something.

That being said, picture this: you're walking down the halls of an ivy-covered institution of higher learning, or perhaps the robotics-parts aisle at the local Radio Shack. You see a man of average build, with shocking Einsteinian white hair and round tortoiseshell spectacles, from behind which peer magnified round blue eyes. There is a brushy mustache and a toothy grin. The man is dressed in vintage nutty-professor wear: tweed jacket, detached suede elbow patches, wrinkled chinos cuffed over Converse Jack Purcell sneakers. A carefully constructed, haphazard disheveled state. This man is the mad scientist right out of central casting. Now tell me, does your mind jump to "God, what a catch!"? Or do you think, "What the hell is the six-foot redhead in the sexy dress doing with him?" Well, in either case, it was—and is—love. Peter once told me that he had been waiting his entire life for me to come along. As the beige spirits predicted, I had no choice in the matter—he is my destiny.

THEN AGAIN, MRS. SHELTON MIGHT HAVE HAD A POINT. ONE DAY I was paging through the arts section of the newspaper and spotted a sure loser.

"Oh, look," I told Peter, "another all-star-cast movie. Those never work. Something called *The Women*."

"*The Women?*" he asked, looking up at me through his

glasses. "That's not new. It's a remake of the 1939 classic starring Joan Crawford, Rosalind Russell, Norma Shearer, and Joan Fontaine."

"How do you know that?" I asked, stunned by his offhanded remark, and not a little scared by the list of women— gay icons, each in her own way.

"How do you not?" he said, a small amount of disdain in his voice. I reflected on how his mother once told me he was "light on his feet."

"He's one of the boys, you know," she imparted. "One of the *boys.*"

Well, thank God he's also a pyromaniac, because his utter love of all things incendiary marks him as completely not gay. Whenever we travel through states where fireworks are legal, he stops at the roadside stands and stocks up. He keeps a stash in the basement of our country house and brings a few out on special occasions. On Truman's birthday, a rocket Peter had lit took off flying on the horizontal, aimed squarely at Peter. He caught the noise over his shoulder and immediately started running through the field. In his defense, the rocket did look as though it were heat seeking. We all watched from the house, laughing hysterically as he ran like a girl to avoid the explosion of color. He later claimed that he was going for the laugh, but he wasn't very convincing, sweating and huffing as though he'd just run a marathon of fear. Okay, maybe not *completely* not gay.

I have found a way to use some of Peter's, let us say, more feminine traits to my advantage. He is always willing to help me with the design of a dress, and he is never leery of carrying my purse at a party, he is so secure in his manhood, or lack thereof. I think he secretly likes the sparkle of the tiny Judith Leiber clutch against his old Rat Pack black tuxedo. Even more amazing, though, is his complete lack of hesitation when I send him out for tampons or yeast infection cures.

"Here," he says, handing me a bag. "I got you the Monistat three-day capsules with the external cream, and the one-day treatment from Vagisil that comes with the cool comfort wipes. I wasn't sure which you'd want, and they both sounded like viable possibilities."

I've always been aware of how much smarter Peter is than pretty much everyone around him, including his wife and off-spring. I used to chalk this up to the age difference (eighteen years, but who's counting), but lately I've had to admit that he is simply always right. I have come to accept this truth, which makes it no less annoying. Because he is smart, he assumed his children would be as well. He was a bit disappointed when the test scores started rolling in.

"Sorry," I said, handing him a pre-k admissions score sheet. "I'm average. I diluted your gene pool."

This houseful of average doesn't bother me at all. I have seen many a person with a genius IQ have difficulty navigating day-to-day life. Peter is one of these types, always misplacing things and being mildly disappointed in the world around him. It can't be easy for him, and if he were a people person, I'm sure it would bother him more. He has wonderful social skills, but prefers not to use them. Peter's carefully cultivated "crazy professor" demeanor is an attempt to ward off normal discourse, particularly with strangers. He also has this way of looking at you with crazy horse eyes, which is sort of off-putting at parties.

I recently read about prosopagnosia, a brain malfunction that interferes with facial recognition. Peter has this. We can be at a party thrown in his honor, stocked with blood relatives and lifelong friends, and he will still tug my sleeve and whisper "Who is that?" in my ear as a colleague of twenty years walks up to us to say hello. I have to say "Hi, *David,* how are things at the *Architectural Digest*? Peter just *loved* the spread on the *Ford project*. Didn't you, dear?" We've got it down to a Mad Libs formula, where the sentence is pretty much the same, and I just fill in the personalizing blanks. If I go too far away from Peter, he pinches my arm. I like to think of it as a love bite.

Peter doesn't rely only on his scary eyes and wacky hair to excuse him from being social; for many years, he used smoking. It worked brilliantly—he could step out of a conversation or a meeting, or exit between courses at a boring dinner party, and hide away for the eight minutes it took to drag one down. He had this funny little habit of putting out a cigarette by rolling the cherry off the end. He then put the butt in his pocket; by the end of the day his clothes would be full of stinking shriveled trash. One day he was in a meeting with clients when little twirls of smoke started coming out of his pocket. A smoldering butt had combusted and ignited the accumulated garbage. When Peter realized what was happening, he tried to get up and leave, but by then his jacket was on full-tilt-boogie fire and he was fast becoming a ball of tweed and flames. His clients started screaming in Italian, as Italians are prone to do, running at him and patting him down as someone else threw a glass of water at his chest. This was the man responsible for building their corporate headquarters. Talk about a career on fire.

PETER HAS GROWN ACCUSTOMED TO BEING MISTAKEN FOR THE boys' grandfather when he's out with them. He may be old enough, technically, but he does not sit on a hill smoking a

pipe, watching me child-mind from afar. He is lithe and ener-
getic, and a natural athlete. Peter has perfect posture and extremely elegant hands. He is so graceful that he can make
bowling look like ballet. But for all his finesse, he is fiercely
competitive. There is no such thing as a friendly game of cro-
quet for Peter, and we have learned not to play board games
with him because of this drive to be on top.

But unlike some younger fathers, who are still building
their careers, Peter never hesitates to put us first. Yes, he does
card tricks, he runs like a girl, he has an überannoying habit of
overintellectualizing everything. But he never complains about
the cost of my shoes; for that alone, he is a keeper. I love the
fact that, as an older father, Peter has his work/family priorities
firmly in place.

One day a few years ago I was in Union Square with Peik
and Truman after school. They were with their skateboarding
pack, executing jumps and spins and other death- and police-
defying acts of wonder. Truman, being five, was drifting into
the larger space of his big brother, and acting very much like
an eight-year-old in every way, until Peik had had enough of
sharing his friends and boxed Truman out. Not one to sulk,
Truman looked around for new fun and noticed a troupe of
break-dancers getting warmed up. He loves break-dancers,
and we often go on adventures in the subways at night to
watch them perform. Knowing what was about to happen, I
got out my phone.

"Peter," I said, "you have to get to Union Square with
your video camera. Truman is about to dance."

"I'm in a meeting with the lawyer."

"Really, Peter. Believe me. You must get this on film."

"I'll be right there."

By the time he arrived, Truman was being introduced to the crowd as part of the crew. The dancers lined up one by one to take their solos. Sure enough, they sent Truman out for his turn. Truman stepped forward in his preppie rugby shirt and carrot-orange hair and executed a series of spins and worms and even the Michael Jackson crotch grab. I laughed until I cried, watching that performance. Peter was thrilled to have preserved the moment. He looked up at me and mouthed, "Thank you."

I pointed down at my new alligator Manolos and mouthed, "Oh no, thank you."

"All my kids' therapists say they are very
well-adjusted."

HELP WITH THE HEAVY LIFTING

SIX KIDS? AND YOU WORK? HOW DO YOU DO IT?

"Well, our oldest is away at college, so there are only five left at home" is how I usually deflect the astonishment from people I meet on the street. "And we have help."

"Oh, you have *help*."

This is where the problem lies. Perhaps people assume that if I have help, then I must be rich, and hating rich people has become the latest American pastime, so they must hate me. Or perhaps because my life was made very public for a short time, during which I was nicknamed "Bad Mommy," they think that this gives them the right to judge my choices.

In any case, people love to beat me up over the fact that I have help. Being raised with nannies doesn't seem to have adversely affected my kids at all. In fact, all their therapists say they are very well adjusted.

In an otherwise innocuous interview for Parents.com, during which I spoke about how I juggle work and family, I mentioned the girls who help me with my children. In the South, where I come from, "girl" is a term of endearment. I call all women "girl," regardless of age, race, or sometimes gender. This tidbit was buried in a five-screen click-through about style and girdles and whatnot, but for some reason Jezebel.com, a women's website that is part of the Gawker group, linked to the article with a squib about how disrespectful it was of me to refer to professional child-care workers as girls. I'd been targeted by this particular website before, so I wasn't taken aback by the hostility. What did surprise me was how many of Jezebel's readers are stay-at-home moms, who actually have the time to read, post, and then have lengthy conversations among themselves about how bad I suck as a mom. Who's watching their kids? The hatred spewed from keyboards all across America.

> SuperSally: If you can't take care of your kids without almost round the clock help from multiple individuals then WTF? Either you had too many damn kids and didn't bother to think about it as you were popping them out or you are incompetent.

Experiencing the pain of childbirth does not make me love my children more; that's why God invented epidurals. Changing every diaper, cooking every meal, and doing every pick-up and drop-off will not make me love them more, either. Choosing not to do so hardly makes me incompetent.

And then there was this type:

Pureblarney: I cry inside every time I wait for the subway next to a child and his nanny. I will be raising my kids, thankyouverymuch, even if I have to pull teeth to keep any semblance of a career in tow.

Awww. You've got to love an idealist willing to perform unlicensed dental procedures for the sake of being with her kids. But would she rather see a totally stressed-out mom pushed to the brink of frustration? A dicey thing if said mom is standing on the edge of a subway platform.

Other comments were virulent—one reader even went so far as to post a testimonial saying she had seen me calmly sit by as my children terrorized an airport terminal. She included in her story the details that my kids were tackling and baiting each other, that I occasionally slung a curse at them, and that Peter was detached and "had completely given up on his family and quite possibly life itself." She did go on to mention in a later comment that the boys were well behaved on the plane, but she never considered that perhaps I was operating from a plan.

Best (or maybe worst) of all, she accused me of dressing the boys in various hues of Polo Ralph Lauren shirts. I ask you, why would I ever spend good money on something like that when L. L. Bean features just as many colors for half the price? Doesn't that nice lady know what kind of shoes I could buy with the difference?

Now I am certainly no stranger to angry comments. I take full responsibility for everything I say and the wrath that comes along with it; I just didn't expect a website that once featured a blogger called Slut Machine to go so self-righteous and judgmental on a woman because she has help. I guess I should be thankful the folks at Jezebel aren't calling me Sexto-mom.

Trust me, I'm not at the spa while someone else is raising my brood. Kids in New York need planned activities; they don't just run out to the backyard or meet up with the neighborhood gang for a game of kick the can. There are music lessons and organized sports, pediatrician and orthodontist appointments, birthday parties, and playdates. Inevitably these events take place at different ends of Manhattan at the same time. It's a complex matrix of times and places, requiring a team effort to make it happen.

If our household is a team, Alicia is the captain.

"Don't forget to pick up Truman after your meeting because Nicole will be with Pierson at reading. I spoke to Peik. He is coming home on his own. I'll take Larson to speech and meet you back here at four-thirty."

Roger that. Dependable and organized, Alicia calls the plays by telling us all where we need to be on any given day. She expertly handles as many as ten speech and language sessions a week for Larson's learning disability; she knows all the therapists' names and has friended them on Facebook. I can count on one hand the days of work she has missed in the thirteen years she has been with our family. I think it's wonderful that my children love this woman, who has cared for them since they were babies. And if she felt disrespected by being referred to as "girl," would she still be here after so many years?

Alicia is a single mother to two boys, Warren and Christian, who have grown up alongside my boys. My philosophy is that if Alicia is happy, I am happy, so I attempt to make her life as stress-free as possible. Having her boys around where she can keep an eye on them makes life easier for all of us. Of course, this puts the boy count in the house at seven on most afternoons. Scan the loft and you will see scattered about the apartment glassy-eyed boys of various sizes and colors planted and staring into screens of some version of mind-sucking technology. Until, of course, they all decide it's time for a game of monkey in the middle. Then they pound about until the downstairs neighbor starts beating on the pipes.

Alicia is petite, well spoken, and well dressed. She never hesitates to use her knowledge of style on me, saying things like "You're not going to leave the house in that, are you? You look like Secretarial School Barbie." Or "Explain to me why you are wearing a tuxedo at two o'clock in the afternoon." Thanks to an addiction to exercise and fitness magazines, she is superfit. When she arrives at eight-thirty in the morning, she has already been to Boot Camp or kickboxing or on some other blood-rushing, muscle-building endeavor. She has a passion for designer handbags and can describe in detail the latest It bag. Once, when I was pitching a fashion game show to a network and needed a display of designer loot to demonstrate the game, I turned to Alicia to borrow what I needed.

"That Chloé bag is gorgeous," said a network executive.

"I know, don't you love it? I borrowed it from my nanny."

"Your nanny? I want to be your nanny."

"Oh, no you don't."

DESPITE HER QUIET DEPENDABILITY, ONE LOOK AT HER FACEBOOK profile photo gives you a clue that Alicia has a wild side. Wearing a wig and a fitted hot-pink dress, photographed from behind showing off her well-toned rear: this is the Alicia I see only occasionally.

"Is that Alicia?" a father asked me at a school Halloween party.

"Catwoman? Yeah, that's her." I smiled.

"That's my sexy nanny!" Pierson added, proud to be there with the masked girl in the tight leather pants carrying a whip. Costume parties always bring out Alicia's wild side. She tends to look like one of the girls on the Leg Avenue packages at Ricky's. The sexy cigarette girl. The glamour gladiator. The dark angel. Every costume features Alicia's hard-earned abs.

She doesn't get mad often, but when she does she is capable of a crippling silent treatment, which renders me defenseless. The silent treatment is the worst for me. Yell at me, hit me, just get it over with. I have tried to convince her that keeping her anger in is unhealthy, and it would better and more cleansing for her to express why she is angry, but I think she knows I am just saying that because I can't bear her torture.

Alicia has been a part of our family as long as Peik has. And when I say "a part" I don't mean some organ we could live without if necessary, like the spleen. Not one of my sons knows a world without her. She knows everyone's favorite snacks and makes sure they are stocked in the pantry. She is the softy in the house: the boys go to her when they feel unloved or in need of some extra attention. To be democratic, she refers to them all as "Boyfriend." When Peik was a baby, he pronounced Alicia "Sheesha," which has stuck so completely that even my friends and neighbors think that is her name.

"I called the house and spoke to Sheesha yesterday," Larson's class mother told me, "She is so lovely. She said it would be no problem to make her banana bread for the bake sale." They know better than to ask me.

Larson has improved upon this moniker by adding "Mom," as in "Sheesha Mom," and sometimes just plain "Mom."

"You are Lawa," he tells me, "and Sheesha is Mom." When he calls out "Mom!" from somewhere in the house, if I respond he will sometimes say, "Not you, Mom, my other mom."

That my children have no problem letting me know exactly on which side their mommy bread is buttered doesn't bother me at all. I've known women who have fired nannies for less-obvious attachment, but my feeling is that if I'm going to entrust my children to another woman, I'm glad they love her. And she, unquestionably, after all these years, loves them right back.

WHEN I MARRIED PETER, ZOILA WAS IN THE PRE-NUP. OR AT LEAST, she would have been if there had been a pre-nup. The first time I came up to Peter's apartment, I couldn't help but notice that he already had a wife: there she was, putting away the laundry.

"Laura, this is Zoila," he told me as she was pulling on her coat and I was taking mine off. "She knows where the bodies are buried."

Nice job description, I thought.

"Nice to meet you, Miss Laura," she said. I liked her instantly. She wears ankle socks, and a cardigan, and she changes her sneakers for Dearfoams slippers when she is in the house. The woman is standard-issue sitcom—Alice from *The Brady Bunch,* with a Guatemalan accent.

"Mr. Peter, I picked up your shirts and bought some new vacuum cleaner bags—and here." She handed him a little pile of business cards, receipts, and what looked like pennies wrapped in lint. "From the laundry."

After Zoila left, Peter explained to me that he'd been see-ing her for nearly twenty years. She had outlasted every girl-friend, casual date, and broken betrothal. Some women had objected to his deep connection with Zoila, claiming that they, too, could starch a collar or take a complete message, with area code, should he not be at home to receive a call. Those women are history; Zoila remains.

"So you see," he told me, "she's part of the deal. If you have a problem with another woman going through my pants and maybe even keeping secrets from you, then you might as well tell me now."

"Can she cook?" I asked. "Because I don't."

"No, she's not a cook," he said. "But I don't really eat."

"She can stay."

This was a smart move on my part, as in all my years of marriage I have never had to remember a thing that involves my husband. People tell me it must be nice to have a house-keeper, but I prefer to think of her as a Peterkeeper. She doesn't run my household, just his Elba-like piece of it.

But Zoila's value to me is also immeasurable: she never forgets a child's birthday (and has even had to remind me a few times), but, most important, she has never, ever told me anything about Peter that I might not want to know. I'm not saying that there's anything to tell, but I gain peace of mind from the confidence that I wouldn't have to bother with it if there were.

WHEN I CRAWLED HOME, PREGNANT AND EXHAUSTED, FROM THE challenge part of *Project Runway,* I was faced with the seem-ingly insurmountable task of creating a twelve-piece collec-tion in two months all by myself. No pattern makers, no cutters, no beaders, just me. This was going to be a full-time task, and I knew that the boys would be too much for Alicia without me, so she brought in Nicole. Now I can't imagine our house without her.

The only thing Alicia and Nicole have in common is that they are both from the Caribbean. While Alicia is petite, Nicole is six feet tall and weighs two hundred pounds, most of it pure muscle. I like to introduce her as my bodyguard.

Every week she shows up with an intricate hairstyle involving hair that is not her own. She seems to think no one knows it is a weave.

"Hey, Nicole, did you hear about the woman who was shot in the head but saved by her weave?" I tease.

"I wouldn't know about a weave," she replied with a gold-capped smile. I *think* that was her reply, anyway. I can't understand a damn thing she says through her heavy Trinidad-via-Brooklyn accent.

Nicole also has a thing for Baby Phat clothing, and a severe case of body dysmorphic disorder. A dangerous combination because Baby Phat tends toward the hoochie side. Whereas most women who suffer from this affliction think they are three sizes larger than they are, Nicole insists on fitting her size 16 body into size 6—the result being endless repairs of burst seams on my machine. She always blames the low quality of the garments.

"Ah, Laura," she said one day, "do you like my new jeans?"

"What?"

"Do you like my new jeans?"

"What?"

"My . . . jeans . . . they . . . are . . . new."

"Oh. You do know they're way too small, right? And why do they have a big metallic cat on the ass?"

"No, Laura, these jeans are so loose," Nicole said, point-ing to her backside. "I should have gotten a smaller size."

"Nicole, look how stressed the seams are in the thighs—they're going to burst."

"That's just because one of my thighs is swollen. It's tem-porary."

"Your thighs are exactly the same." I get out my measur-ing tape to prove it to her. "It's those tight jeans, cutting off your circulation."

If Alicia is the captain of our family, then Nicole is the en-forcer. At six o'clock, she lines up all the boys and makes them eat. At seven o'clock, she lines them up and makes them bathe. At eight o'clock, brush teeth; nine o'clock, bedtime. While Alicia will always give you a snack—sometimes one she's already eating—Nicole will glower and point you in the direction of the kitchen, where she has prepared six different dishes, some of which resemble cat food and all of which are so inedible that the kids cry, begging for cereal. We always hope that Alicia has found some time during the day to cook.

The enforcer is very protective.

"When I was leaving school today, one of the mothers asked me who picks the boys' clothes," Nicole recounted. It is true that besides Pierson, my other boys always look like they just stepped out of a Salvation Army dollar bin.

"What did you say?" I asked.

"I just kept walking so I wouldn't have to answer with my fist."

While Nicole rules the kids with an iron fist and a gold grille, her personal life is a circus. Her phone rings constantly with calls from family members in crisis. There are always lawsuits and court dates, shootings and evictions, deaths and financial crises. Her entire family went to visit her brother in prison and she came back with a group photo to show the kids.

"This is my brother," she said, pointing to a large man in the center.

"Why is he wearing an orange jumpsuit?" Larson asks, never one to miss a costume.

"That's what they make you wear in prison." She continued: "This is my mother and my sister. And this is my brother's son, Jayden."

"Your whole family is in jail? Even the kids?"

THANKS TO MY GIRLS, MY HUSBAND, AND MY OWN CONSIDERABLE contributions, our schedule runs like a many-geared, well-oiled machine. During the week, Peter gets the boys up and fixes them breakfast while I get them dressed. Then he takes the three oldest off to school and either heads to work or comes back home. Larson and Finn hang with me until Alicia arrives. She fixes Larson's lunch and takes him to school, and I watch Finn while I get dressed. When she gets back, I get to work, whatever that may entail for the day. Alicia will place grocery orders and unpack the boxes, and (we hope) cook, to spare us from Nicole's cooking. If the weather is nice, she will take Finn to the park. When school ends, everyone begins to pinball around the city. Nicole starts work at three o'clock. She goes straight to school and picks up Truman and Pierson on Mondays and drops off Truman at his reading tutor while she and Pierson shop. These shopping excursions may include a stop at the man on Fourteenth Street who fits you for a grille: Pierson is waiting for his second front tooth to come in to get his. On Wednesdays and Fridays, Nicole picks up Pierson early to take him to his reading tutor and I pick up Truman. I usually forget and arrive late at school to find Truman in the lobby, greeting me with some comment like "What the fuck just happened here?" Zoila comes to clean for a few hours on Mondays and Wednesdays. Meanwhile, Alicia takes Finn to pick up Larson, and either brings him home for an in-house speech session with Craig or takes him to his other speech therapist, Amy. Peik usually has to be tracked down on Mondays and Wednesdays to get him home on time for Sabina, his homework helper. On Tuesdays and Thursdays, Nicole brings Truman and Pierson to me, I take them to fencing, and Nicole watches Finn so Alicia can go home. When we get back, Nicole watches Finn and Larson and reads with Pierson, while I help Peik and Truman with their homework. When Peter gets home, he helps them with the math that I can't do. Nicole puts the three smallest ones to bed, then goes home. This leaves Peter and me to get the big boys to bed on time so we can catch a few hours of sleep before musical beds begins.

The fact that all these children have all these places to be is actually the easy part. Getting there is the hard part. There is no SUV parked in the driveway ten feet from the kitchen door. These children are not conveniently delivered door to door in the safety of their car seats. We perform a balancing act involving taxis, buses, subways, strollers, and Snuglis.

Taxis can be difficult to get, especially if the weather is bad, and as the meter ticks up, your bank account ticks down. Buses tend to have older passengers with little patience for a crying child. Nicole once got into an argument with a patron complaining about Larson that ended in the bus driver pulling over and the man fleeing. Subways present an array of problems. While they are undoubtedly the fastest way to get around Manhattan, they are not handicap friendly, and traveling with a child in a stroller is basically the same as wheeling around an invalid.

Alicia was once in a subway station on her way to pick up Cleo from school; she had four-year-old Peik in a stroller. When they got to the turnstile, she asked Peik to get out of the stroller so she could maneuver it through. He did as he was asked and went through the turnstile just as the next train was pulling up to the platform. The doors opened and he stepped in. The doors closed and the train pulled away. Unfortunately, Alicia watched the entire scene from the turnstile, where she was wedged in by the menacing Maclaren.

Resourcefully, she picked up the nearby emergency phone and had a calm conversation with a dispatcher. The transit people told her to wait at that station; the police would apprehend the little escapee at the next station and bring him back to her. Within a few minutes, Alicia had Peik back, safe and sound. She wasn't even late to pick up Cleo.

When she returned home, she burst into tears in a delayed panic attack and fearfully recounted the story. She was sure she would be fired.

"What will Peter say?" she blurted between sobs.

"Peter will say he had no idea there were emergency phones in the subway. Peter will say he was glad it happened with you and not me, because you handled it so well. Peter will say you deserve a bonus."

WE MAY HAVE PLENTY OF HELP DURING THE WEEK, BUT UNTIL RE- cently Peter and I were full-time parents on the weekends. As much as I hated being stuck in the kitchen preparing three seven-person meals a day, I have to admit that Peter had the more difficult task. The amount of activity required to keep the boys occupied when they don't have school is immense.

"I need a youth replacement," Peter said, exhausted on the sofa one Sunday evening after a marathon of boy activities. "I'm old; I can't do this every weekend." He was right. Hide-and-seek, bike riding, swimming, skiing, catch—the man needed some downtime. He worked hard all week and worked even harder on the weekends.

Blake first introduced himself to me in the lobby of my big kids' school. He had no idea we were looking for a manny.

"Hi, Laura, I'm Blake. I just wanted to tell you what a big fan I am of your work." I'm never surprised by the variety of people who watch *Project Runway.* I meet a lot of men who watch it with their daughters or wives, so a man in his thirties didn't set off any alarms.

"Thanks, Blake. What are you doing here?" I wasn't sure whether he was a young father or a teacher.

"I've worked with a family for many years whose boys go here. They're grown now, and don't really need me anymore, but I try to get by at least once a week and spend some time with them."

"What do you do now?" I asked, suddenly registering the possibility that all my weekend dreams might be about to come true.

"I'm a professional dancer and I teach dance at a school uptown."

I liked how strong Blake looked, and how calm, and he obviously had quite a bit of experience taking care of boys. I could easily see him keeping my pack well entertained. He got the job without even knowing he was being interviewed. We had found our manny.

"Oh, and I'm gay," he said, as we shook hands on the deal.

"Perfect," I replied. "So's my husband."

Blake is just as likely to teach the boys how to build a treehouse as how to sing an aria or how to execute a perfect pirouette—a versatility that has earned him the handle Butch Ballerina. He will drive the boys off to Rye Playland on a Saturday, and be right back at it on Sunday morning to set up soccer pitches and kick a damn ball up and down the field with them. He will then come inside, don an apron, and whip up a meal. Most of his recipes rely on some flavor of Campbell's Cream of Something Soup, from the classic tuna noodle hot dish to the more exotic Broccoli Cheese chicken casserole. Whatever the dish, Blake presents it with a flourish, as though he hadn't just opened a can of glop and poured it over a dead bird. He is undoubtedly more David than Amy Sedaris, but any meal he cooks is one less meal I have to deal with.

While for most of the weekend his butch side dominates, the ballerina side of Blake sometimes rears its precious head. He often complains about the temperature in the car and can be fussy about his clothes. Often before he leaves for the ski slope with the boys he will run back into the house from the car to change his coat.

"This coat is ugly; I can't be seen in it," he'll whine.

"Really? Because at least that one didn't make your butt look big," I tease. Five minutes later, he'll back for a second change of coat.

Blake's gayness fascinates my boys. If he mentions that he thinks the new girl serving burgers at the Red Rooster is pretty, they will tell him, "You're not really gay, you like girls." They're always asking him when he "turned gay" and why he "decided to be gay." But their all-time favorite method of

Blake torture is to sing a small clip from a song in the *Family Guy* episode where the family inherits a mansion in Newport, Rhode Island, from Lois's rich aunt. Petah is singing "This House Is Freakin' Sweet" which includes the line "One hundred bucks, Blake is gay." They sing it over and over, laughing hysterically, proud that Seth McFarlane wrote it just for them. Blake always handles these incidents with patience and understanding.

Blake will do practically anything a child will do, and with the kind of enthusiasm that makes you think he's enjoying it. He takes them to man movies I don't want to see, builds fire pits in the woods, and makes them bows and arrows out of tree branches. He is a walking Dangerous Book for Boys.

I once came upon him with Pierson and Peik out behind the house. Truman was standing a good distance away.

"Hey, Blake," I said, "what are you guys doing with my hairspray?"

"Building a potato launcher."

"We're trying to hit Truman," Peik said, holding a length of PVC pipe and a Bic lighter. Pierson had a bowl of potatoes.

"Won't that hurt?" I asked.

"Oh, no," Blake said. "We're using baked potatoes."

"Well, carry on, girls," I said, rolling my eyes, and went off in search of some well-paid-for peace and quiet.

"Being on *Project Runway* was a lot like
childbirth. When you are in the middle of it,
it's painful, but when it's all over,
you're glad you did it."

LAURA'S GOT A GUNN

BOUT SIX YEARS AGO, BETWEEN KIDS NUMBER four and five, I stumbled upon a new obsession: reality television. And not just any reality television. On *Project Runway,* a mixed assortment of completely crazy fashion designers is given little time and less money to craft a runway-worthy garment good enough to get them past the even crazier judges and on to the next week's challenge. It had me at *Auf Wiedersehen.* I loved the characters, the obstacles, and the creativity—and no one had to eat live worms.

I am no stranger to the impossible. Work two jobs, go to grad school, and single-handedly rear my daughter in a city where I know not one soul? Sure, no problem. Find a second husband and give him five boys in ten years, rearing them all in a two-bedroom apartment in the middle of Manhattan while continuing my career as an architect? Don't make me shrug. Create a killer dress from a paper clip and a piece of lint? Freaking *cakewalk.*

I tried to share my love by telling everyone to watch the show with me, but reality television with its lowbrow reputation was too hard a sell in my house—not to mention the part about people sewing dresses. I did manage to convince my nine-year-old, Truman, to sit by my side as I yelled at the screen—disagreeing with the judges' comments or questioning a contestant's design decision—and that was because the show aired past his bedtime. One late night, as I was watching an episode I had already seen at least fourteen times, Truman looked up at me from where he lay.

"That dress should not have been cut on the bias," he muttered. "Mom, you can do better than that."

You're right, I thought. That fabric is not bias friendly. I could do better with my eyes closed. I hadn't been to fashion school, but I had learned to sew when I was tiny, and my architecture training had honed my sense of design to a razor-sharp edge. I'd been making fantastic, elegant black-tie-event dresses for years; I knew how to drape and make patterns without ever really thinking about it. As I sat on the couch, Truman gently snoring during the runway segment, it occurred to me that I could audition for the next season. What was there to lose? At least if I got cast all my friends and family would have to watch the show with me, even if I didn't make it very far.

I found the New York City open call on the Bravo website—it was to be held in three days. I couldn't believe my luck. The interviews would be at Macy's, only three blocks away, so I wouldn't have to travel or make any crazy arrangements for the kids. It really was a no-brainer.

I wasn't sure what they would be looking for, so I decided to bring what I do best, grabbing three sparkling cocktail dresses from the clothing rack in my bedroom. I was flying blind, trying to remember what contestants had shown up with in the past and gleaning what I could from the Internet. I figured my chances were about as slim as those of an African American ever becoming president, but then again, why *not* me? I can out-gay the gayest young male designer out there, I told myself. The night before the auditions, I ignored the March forecast of "continued cold snap" and selected a shimmery sleeveless cocktail dress lush with hand beading and a neckline that plunges to the navel. When I pulled it on the next morning, I hoped I would stand out from the crowd.

And I do mean crowd. Peter walked with me, and when we showed up at the side entrance of Macy's the line of people stretched all the way down Thirty-fourth Street and wrapped around the world's most famous department store.

Peter, my hero, offered to hold my place in line so I could return home and wait in our warm apartment. God, I love that man. He called me hours later saying he was getting close to the front and it was time to make the switch.

Just as I arrived at Peter's place in line, a guy with the requisite gear and a clipboard—clearly a producer—came outside for the next ten contestants.

"Seven, eight, nine," he counted out, and when he said, "Ten," I felt a hand on my shoulder guiding me through the door. My sense of the surreal started to kick into high gear.

Once inside the waiting room, I took off my coat and smoothed my hair, ignoring the nine people staring at me like

I was crazy to wear a beaded dress before noon. Dress like you want it or stay home, I thought as I refreshed my red lipstick. They kept staring. I guess when you spend hours on a city street in the freezing cold a bit of camaraderie develops. I didn't quite have that frozen-to-near-death-camped-on-the-sidewalk look about me. I had more like a spent-the-night-clubbing-at-the-Ritz-in-my-fancy-black-cocktail-dress look.

When it was my turn, the producers switched on my mic and told me to enter the room with my dresses and portfolio and stand on the X on the floor. I was specifically told not to try to shake anyone's hand, which I found disappointing as by now I had a major crush on Tim Gunn and very much wanted a chance to touch him. It wasn't a physical thing at all, really. I had just gained so much respect for his design aesthetic that I needed to make sure he was real. The more I thought about my infatuation, the more sense the no-handshaking rule made.

Once in the room, everything went by in a blur. I was operating on the adrenaline high of my life. Tim thumbed through my book and asked if I had made the dresses myself. I nodded meekly, or maybe I spoke a few words in the affirmative. I was so stunned to be standing there with the cameras rolling that I lost all sense of this being a competition—I really felt as though I had somehow already won just by getting in the door. I half expected to be thanked and sent on my way, and was already concocting the dinner-party small talk this episode of my life would soon be reduced to. It was then that I noticed people off to one side of the room—likely network executives or the big producers of the show—waving their arms at the judges and mouthing "Take the crazy lady in the cocktail dress." Yes, I thought, you should take the crazy lady in the cocktail dress. Tim seemed less interested in my dramatic potential than in my garments—were they up to snuff? The next thing I knew, they told me I had made it to round two. I'd like to think it was my cleavage that got me the gig, but there's not really enough of it. It's much more likely that bedazzling oneself for an eight A.M. audition was exactly the kind of nutty behavior that reality television thrives on. At least for a couple of episodes.

I arrived home a mere hour after I had left, frozen and gleeful. I announced to the gathered sleepy faces that I had made it through to the next round. My next task was to make a three-minute bio video to send to Los Angeles. I had exactly one day to figure out how the hell I was going to make it on the show. Peter was thrilled by the whole prospect, and immediately took charge.

"If we shoot footage today," he said, "we can edit it tomorrow and get it to FedEx by nine P.M. That should get it to L.A. in time."

Since the odds were good that the producers wanted me because I stood out, we decided that the video should be about my personality and not about fashion. We began constructing our theme: older glamorous urban woman with a scary number of children. We did our best to set me apart from all the young gay designers fresh out of fashion school. Peter shot me in the center of a dizzying, death-defying, high-speed video of our loft, complete with four boys running around, a swinging skeleton chandelier above, my pet tortoise, a massive cage full of birds, and of course the dress forms and sewing machines behind me, a subtle homage to the requisite "interview shot" from the show itself. I meanwhile stood placidly in the center of this storm and confidently claimed that the breakneck speed of *PR* would be like a vacation for me.

It was a mad dash to FedEx but the video went off in time, and at that point. I waited eagerly to hear back from the producers whether or not I had been chosen. No word came. Weeks passed. Hamsters were born and died. The seasons changed. There was nothing to do, and no one to call. The wait was excruciating. Then one May evening my cell phone rang. The screen read "unlisted number."

"Laura, this is Tim Gunn," the unmistakable voice said.

"Tim Gunn?" I practically screamed. He gave me the good news and asked me to keep it a secret—apart from my neighbors, who must have heard my shout. Filming would start in two weeks. I began to prepare for what would be the most unreal reality of my life.

After I hung up and the initial shock wore off, I realized I had two problems: my daughter, Cleo, was due to graduate from high school during sequestered shooting, and I was about eight weeks pregnant. I might already have been knocked up at the audition, but it seemed so unlikely that I would get to the second round, much less be cast, that I conveniently ignored my compromised condition. I instantly made up my mind that I would put Cleo first if she wanted me to, and that nothing I did for the show could imperil the baby. I'd had five uncomplicated pregnancies at this point, and could certainly tell whether anything was amiss. I decided not to mention the bun in the oven until absolutely necessary, assuming that productions of this scale have certain liability concerns—I worried that if the producers knew they would replace me at this point in the game. On the other hand, if I made it through enough rounds to start showing, they would have to work the pregnancy in, like when a soap opera star has to spend three months of shooting behind a potted plant, or is "suddenly impregnated by her own evil twin."

I called Cleo, who had been just as nervously waiting to hear from Tim as I had been. She was thrilled.

"I'll miss your graduation," I said, heartsick at the words. "It's your choice. If you want me there, I will turn down the show."

"Are you nuts?!" she yelled at me. "This is so exciting! You *have* to do it."

With Cleo's blessing, I moved ahead and followed the shows orders to the letter, and prepared my family for my departure. The older boys were happy to see me go: Peik because he was always happy to see me go anywhere, and Truman because he was my partner in crime. The younger two didn't really get it—being three and four, they hadn't yet grasped the concept of time—and I knew that their collective amnesia would pave over any hurt feelings in the long run. I packed a couple of suitcases and my own sewing kit, and moved into an apartment six blocks from my home. I could literally see the boys' bedroom window from mine. We could have used a flashlight to communicate, if they'd only known where I was.

Moving into the apartment with its tiny bedrooms and even tinier bathroom was a snap after my six-people-to-two-bedrooms lifestyle. Many of the other contestants were used to living in houses and had trouble getting to sleep in the middle of noisy Manhattan. I had that edge from the beginning, as I am indifferent to regular sleep patterns—and can fall asleep practically anywhere and wake on a dime. Years of babies do that to you: I haven't slept through the night in ten years. I wear sleep deprivation like a navel-baring cocktail dress—anywhere, anytime.

Our first challenge started the minute we walked into our apartment: make an outfit out of something in the suite. For as much as I had been looking forward to the challenges, tearing apart my apartment was not exactly a thrill, especially when we returned exhausted to the demolished apartment that night, one designer already *Auf Weidersehen*ed off the show. Though tired, I was proud of my sexy little mattress ticking coat with its bathmat collar: It was the first garment I had ever sewn for someone other than myself. In a way I think that my lack of formal training was an advantage. I wasn't restricted by the "right" way to do things, so I just figured out the fastest or easiest way. Other contestants wouldn't dream of leaving raw edges on the inside of a garment because they had been taught that it was unprofessional. I had no such hangups, and could better spend my time executing more-intricate ideas. As long as my design passed the runway test—does it look good to the judges at thirty paces?—then finishes be damned.

If you think what the designers go through on *Project Runway* looks hard on TV, in real life it's even harder. Trust me. First of all, "this week's challenge" did not give us a week to recover each time. We were given a new assignment every day or two, back to back to back. Remaining creative was nearly impossible at that pace, and it's no wonder that contestants started to crack so early in the competition. I'm not very good at faking how I feel, and since I was newly pregnant and prone to fatigue, my goal in the first few challenges was to keep my head low, design quick, execute quicker, and take a nap while the other designers were fussing over how to properly drape their fabrics. Of all my six pregnancies, this was turning out to be the easiest, and I was determined not to whine or complain about any of my symptoms. I don't get morning sickness, but I do get bone tired, so any bit of sleep I could grab I went for it. This, unfortunately, led to endless footage of me sacked out like a princess. It's not exactly a great way to make friends with a dozen or so people who already want you to go home so they can move up. Luckily, I didn't care a bit what other people thought, and if my ability to get the work done fast made them nervous, so much the better.

The days were long. Work invariably finished at midnight, and then we were woken up at six thirty by a camera in the face and the entire day would start all over again. I exacted a modicum of revenge by sleeping naked and throwing off my covers in the morning just to torture the cameramen.

Elimination days between the challenges were a bit easier physically, but much more draining emotionally. The fifteen-minute runway and judging segment would take the full day to shoot, during which time no one had a clue whether they would be getting *das* boot or not. There was generally a mad dash to finish the garments before it was time to dress the models; then the waiting began. Naturally, there was a camera catching every expression as we all internally freaked out about what might happen on the runway. The minute the elimination segment ended, the next challenge was announced and the gerbil wheel started squeaking all over again. This cycle repeated about a dozen times in a six-week span, and added to it was the minor detail that I was increasingly pregnant.

EVERY TIME HEIDI STOOD ON THE RUNWAY AND INTRODUCED A "SPE-cial guest," I would say to myself, "Please, let it be Peter.

Please, let it be Peter." Was I thinking that there was going to be a "Fashion Inspired by Architecture" challenge and Peter was going to be the guest judge? I was too tired to be rational. For the "Every Woman" challenge Heidi announced that there would be special guests and just as I was saying to myself, "Please, let it be Peter," my mom appeared. I burst into tears. I'm not sure whether I was happy to see my mother or sad not to see Peter, or just being a hormonal, sewing freak of nature, but there she was, along with a mother or sister for every designer on the show.

I would have to say that conceptually this was the worst challenge of the entire season. None of these everyday women knew that they had come to New York to walk on the runway in "designer fashions." They were told that they would be doing interviews about us, sharing stories of how wacky we were as children, and showing pictures of us butt naked on a bearskin rug. Many of the women, especially the larger ones, were uncomfortable with the idea of strutting their stuff on national TV, and they simply weren't prepared to be that emotionally naked. Plus, the designers were all so exhausted by the time our relatives arrived, we were all skating on thin brains. The competition was a combustible situation in the finest of hours, but the combination of body-conscious women and hot-headed designers was lethal. The episode was a bit of a disaster, with the least-svelte women crying on the runway because they were so uncomfortable in what they were wearing—fashion can be cruel that way, but even crueler when the wearer is someone you love.

Reality television is real. The producers never tell you what to say or what to do. They end up with hours of footage from many different cameras, and they will edit and distill personalities for the sake of telling a story, but generally the camera doesn't lie. If Omarosa claims she's really not a bitch, and she was merely edited to look that way, you can rest assured that she really is a bitch. During your waking hours cameras are on and you're miced—it's really not possible to be someone that you're not. You become so accustomed to having a camera in your face you actually forget it's there.

On day two of the Every Woman challenge, we all went to Tavern on the Green as a special treat for the mothers and sisters before they would be completely humiliated on the runway the next day. My mother and I were standing on the brunch buffet line as Michael Kors approached with his mother.

"Mom," he said, "this is Laura and she has five children!" Being an only child, Michael is fascinated by my brood and always introduces me this way.

"Well, I'm actually working on number six," I said, patting my belly. It just slipped out. I had no problem telling a complete stranger I was pregnant, or springing it on the entire production team in such an offhand way, but I had completely forgotten that my mother was standing next to me and that I hadn't yet taken the time to tell her. She stared at me, mouth agape, and took a few seconds to regain her composure.

"What?" she finally managed to croak out. "Oh, Laura. You are not serious!"

By her shock and awe you would have thought I was an unwed teenager under her parents' roof. I'm not sure whether she was horrified about me having yet another baby or about the way she found out, but it made great television. It was just about then, I later learned, that the producers started referring to me as the "story line."

MY PERSONAL LEAST FAVORITE PART OF THE SHOW WAS FLYING TO Paris. Under any other circumstances, I would have been thrilled to have a first-class ticket to Paris. Everyone else was so excited, I'm sure I looked like an ingrate, but it just felt wrong not to tell my husband I was leaving the country. And, let's face it, flying over the ocean is no treat when you're forty-two and pregnant. I think I left my ankles someplace over Iceland. Once we were in the City of Lights, it wasn't like we could pop open the champagne and enjoy a sidewalk café, two of the best parts of any trip to France. In fact, we spent the entire time indoors, in an unair-conditioned space, during an intense heat wave. Poor Angela, who was by far the most excited to go to Paris, was eliminated practically as soon as she exited customs and had to turn back around.

Our challenge was to make a haute couture outfit, which was then featured on a canal boat on the Seine, the only time we were let out of our dank cave. My dress looked great on the boat, but the starched frill collar apparently soaked up the humid air off the river; by the time it got across the ocean and onto the elimination runway in New York, I was shocked to find myself at the bottom of the group. My dress had been well received in Paris, and it didn't occur to me that the damage done during transport was that significant. Thank God Vincent made an awful upholstery fabric dress that sent him packing; it would have been embarrassing to be sent home with that still up there on the runway.

A couple of challenges later, I made it into the final four, and we were all let out of our prisons for two months to toil on our collections. Thrilled to be out of the company of my captors, I headed straight for Peter's office. I wanted to see him the most. The entire time I was sequestered, people would ask, "Don't you miss your kids?" "Sure, but I miss my husband more" was always my answer. I mean, I knew him first, and he is the person with whom I share the events of my day, the one who helps me solve the problems that overwhelm me. He is the only person who will tell me if my butt looks big. I need him. He had no idea we were being released, so he was considerably surprised to see me waddle into his office. He walked my bloated and exhausted body home and on the way revealed to me that though he didn't know *everything,* he did know quite a bit of what I had been through. He had found a connection. Manhattan is an island after all. Your brother-in-law's housekeeper's sister may be a ticket agent at Delta, or the lady who owns your dry cleaner's ex-husband is the security guard at Parsons. I'm not sure exactly how Peter got his infor-mation, but through the subway grapevine, Peter knew that my mother had visited, and that I had gone to Paris. He knew that I had won only one challenge, and—most important, he said—he knew that the baby and I were fine. He was angry about our sleep schedule, so he had made it a habit to call the production assistant who was in charge of the contestants every morning at five A.M. and hang up, for revenge. He even came to Parsons once, bluffing his way past the security guard and even making it all the way to the workroom, but we were out, possibly digging through garbage for the materials for our next challenge.

I'm constantly asked how, with five kids, I managed all the work required for the show. The truth is, my husband had a much harder time than I did. As contestants, we were com-pletely sequestered until the finale break. There were no sooth-ing phone calls to toddlers or trips to the drugstore. Every contact with the outside world was carefully monitored and recorded, which limited both spontaneity and sentimentality. I'm not really the type to get all blubbery with a camera in my grille. We didn't have any free time to read magazines or watch TV, which was a good thing because we weren't allowed to anyway. For six weeks, Peter completely pulled the weight of the four kids at home. He was father and mother at the same time. By comparison, competing was easy. For the first time in seventeen years, I didn't have to feed or bathe someone else, I didn't have to worry about anyone but myself, and I was the one being taken care of to a great extent. The producers drove us everywhere we needed to go, provided endless food and drink, and even told us when to sleep and when to sew. It was a lot like being a fashion-conscious toddler.

Once liberated, I took a day off to hear about everything that had happened while I was away—who lost how many teeth, what boy hit which kid, who learned to do what at which summer camp—and then set to work, knowing that whatever I was about to create, it would have a lot of hand-work on it that only I could execute. By the time Tim came for his midway visit, I had more than half my garments completed. It was great to see him, though when he warned me that everything was looking "too Laura" I decided I didn't care if I lost as long as everything I made was as beautiful as it could be. It was during this visit that he told me why he had initially quailed at my audition: he didn't believe that I had made those three dresses myself. The work was too intricate, he said, I didn't look like I had the patience to string beads and sew them onto a dress. I laughed, discreetly touching his arm.

"How do you feel now?" I asked him. "Should I sign up for classes at Parsons?"

"Laura"—he looked at me in his trademark semi-serious way—"you could teach classes at Parsons."

"Thanks," I said, suddenly feeling overwhelmed by all that had happened since that first phone call, and with all that was still to come—the finale and the upcoming birth of my sixth child. "I might just do that."

During our shooting hiatus, the show began to air and people started recognizing me on the street. This was totally unexpected, and I was eager for Peter to witness a sighting. One day, instead of going to work, he came with me to Mood Fabrics, a store featured prominently on the show and a place I knew I would score. We spent a good half hour feeling up fabric, and not one person came up to me with the now familiar "Are you Laura from *Project Runway*?" I finally gave up; then, just as we were exiting the store, a woman approached. I nudged Peter to pay attention and put an open look on my face.

"Excuse me," she said, looking at my husband. "Aren't you Peter Shelton, the architect?" So much for budding celebrity.

WHEN WE RECONVENED FOR FASHION WEEK, I WAS SUSPICIOUS OF the intricate finishing work done on Jeffrey's collection. For the most part I got along well with the other contestants, even Jeffrey, who would say nasty things about me in the safety of the interview room but never to my face. He only picked on the weaker contestants in person—or, in the case of the Every Woman challenge, their mothers. Still, we all shared our tools and critiques and generally were pleasant to one another.

Craftsmanship is like a signature, it doesn't change and I felt Jeffrey's garments were not consistent with the work I had seen him do. The other two finalists agreed, and I decided I needed to say something to the producers. If I didn't, I would regret it forever. I am known for my candor and operating without filters, but in this case I carefully considered the ramifications of speaking up and took the burden completely on myself, leaving Michael and Uli out of the equation. Ironically, "Don't cause any trouble" had been the last bit of advice Peter gave me before I left for the finale. But this was not about causing trouble; if I was going to lose, it had to be because I simply wasn't the best. I couldn't accept going down against illicit work.

In the end I was satisfied with the course of action the producers decided was most prudent. Ultimately Jeffrey went on to win the show, and I was pleasantly surprised by how relieved I was by garnering runner-up status; now I wouldn't forever be tied to having been a reality show winner and there would be no pressure to create a full fashion line for the following fall shows. I did feel that Uli was robbed, though; she should rightly have won. If Jeffrey sewed all of his garments himself, then I wish him luck. Otherwise, karma's a bitch.

Someone said to me that not winning could be a real advantage. He was right. I have heard that contestants on *Survivor* get paid $10,000 to participate whether they win or lose. Contestants on *Project Runway* aren't paid a dime. As Heidi would say, you're either in or you're out—of the money, that is. Either you win $100,000 or you go home with an empty bag. And after all, my dream was to watch the show with my friends and family, which for one brief shining season we did, from beginning to bittersweet end.

To satisfy my reality television cravings, I have had to start watching *Top Chef.* I'm not a foodie—I don't cook and I don't even necessarily enjoy eating—but I do love hearing the judges speak about the food and listening to the chefs explain their decisions. As it turns out, cooking is just another design solution, using sunchokes and geoduck instead of satin and chiffon. I'm right back where I started, as my family won't watch with me, but this time I won't be packing my knives and standing in any audition lines.

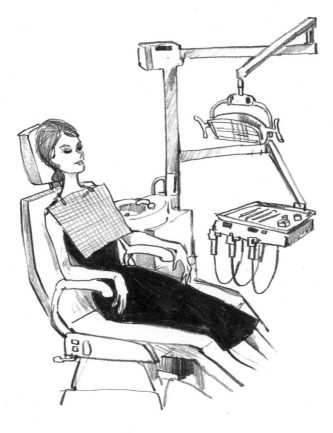

"There's nothing like a root canal to secure
some guilt-free me time."

SIX AND THE CITY

VERY NOW AND THEN, I'LL HAVE ONE OF THOSE days where I walk my feet off all over New York City, chasing down some fabric, picking up one kid, handing off another, meeting with a producer, going on an interview, having lunch with a friend, and dropping a pair of run-down Manolos at shoe rehab. At the end of that kind of day, I will enter my apartment to find at least five children and often twice as many, various adults, an unstable rabbit, and a tortoise named Frank. When I step off the elevator and into this wall of noise, the phrase "Women and children first" usually ticks across my brain, reminding me that there is a chance of rescue. Maybe this happens because the length of the place looks remarkably like the *Titanic,* tipped up on one end and spilling its sliding contents into the swirling subarctic waters below. Or it may just be an involuntary mantra that keeps me from jumping ship. Don't get me wrong, I thrive on being in the center of a chaotic storm—I did grow up in New Orleans, after all.

People expect our home to look like one of my husband's projects, which are featured frequently in magazines like *Architectural Digest.* He has an impeccable eye for simplicity and elegant, understated touches in the spaces he designs. In stark contrast, our loft bears a greater resemblance to *the* projects. I am always amused by the look of surprise when someone comes to our apartment for the first time. Once they've tripped through the obstacle course of scooters and skateboards, backpacks and discarded winter coats around the threshold, they come face-to-face with the one item that defines our space: the sofa.

This sofa was a big purchase for us. It was a special order from one of the fancy upholsterers that my husband uses for his clients, a rich brown leather with real down cushions for extra comfort. We waited four months for it to arrive. I watched nervously as the deliverymen maneuvered it into the freight elevator. When they finally got it into our apartment, I sniffed the air around it, taking in the distinct smell of new. They set it in place and began to unwrap it. Once revealed, the sofa was perfect, gorgeous, a giant Manolo for my ass.

That was twelve years and a few babies ago. The poor thing still sits there, a shred of its former self. The luxurious leather, so soft it was almost suedelike, didn't hold up well to vomit or leaking sippy cups. Within a year, the seat cushions were cracked and torn and I had to make fabric covers for them. When holes began to appear on the arms and backrest, we resorted to the ultimate white-trash fix-all, duct tape. When we were having guests over and trying to make the place look nice, my husband would apply a fresh coat of tape.

Any attempt I have made to have nice furniture has failed miserably in the face of my whirlwind of boys. The pair of Barcelona chairs I dreamt of owning since I studied Mies van der Rohe in architecture school sits deteriorating, buttons gone and foam chunks oozing from the once beautifully tufted leather cushions. In a feat that impressed even me, my kids managed to destroy the matching table, somehow getting the seventy-five-pound piece of glass off its graceful chrome base and smashing it. The Jacobsen swan chairs with their smooth swivel action and hand-upholstered wool seats are now so encrusted with indeterminate substances that the color has turned from a warm red to a unnamable shade of grunge. My tall, slender Mackintosh ladderback chair has been knocked over so many times that the grid is no longer orthogonal. The seventeenth-century fruitwood bombe chest that my husband inherited from his mother now has gouges all over the wood where multiple wheeled objects have repeatedly slammed into it.

It's not just the furniture that has been marked by the destructiveness of my minions. Our once-pristine white walls now have a wainscoting of scribbles at child-height; the blank canvas is just too much for budding artists to resist. Nonremovable stickers of a special industrial grade pepper the windows. Behind every door is a crater where the knob slammed into the sheetrock during a game of chase.

About six years ago, I reluctantly cried uncle and turned the apartment over to the kids. Kitchen appliances are buried beneath notices of field trips past and present, and artwork I can't be caught throwing away. Every television sits in a nest of the tangled miles of cords and controllers it takes to power the various video game systems. Several swings and a punching bag now hang from the ceiling. Overflowing baskets of sporting equipment and bins of headless action figures inhabit every corner. A life-size coffin, perfectly acceptable at Halloween but a bit macabre any other time of the year, serves as a coffee table because we have no place to store it.

Sometime in the future, when my children have homes of their own to destroy, I will have a beautifully furnished apartment. It will be as fabulous as the interiors my husband designs for his clients, with all of the classic twentieth-century furniture I covet. But for now, IKEA is all my kids deserve.

Because the existing furniture is one notch short of disposable, and there is nothing of value left to break, our loft is the perfect place to have big parties. There's our annual Halloween bash. The "Viva Las Vegas" party is admittedly a cliché but still always a favorite, especially when there are at least twenty little kids running around dressed like Elvis. "Party Like a Rock Star" headlined forty kids in faux-hawks with inflatable guitars crammed on a stage lip-synching Led Zeppelin. "If You're Indicted You're Invited" saw an amazing array of favorite criminals, from O. J. Simpson to Jean Harris. Vincent "the Chin" Gigante showed up in his robe, on Heidi Fleiss's arm. One of my personal favorites combined the themes of all the other parties into one name—Michael Jackson. People came as any version of MJ from the little black boy belting "ABC" to the child-molesting plastic-surgery victim dangling a baby off a hotel balcony.

As much fun as this apartment is, it also has its drawbacks. It's an open-plan loft, so we basically live in one big room. There are two bedrooms, one large and one small. The large one is filled with bunk beds that are not specifically assigned. First come, first served—if you want to sleep on the bottom, then go to bed first. The smaller bedroom harbors Peter, the baby, and me, but not always in that order.

Because the bedrooms leave little space for activities other than sleeping, everything else—with the exception of bathroom things—happens out in the open, and often we are in a state of Too Much Information.

Finding space around here can prove challenging. I wind up hiding in that fallback safe haven, the bathroom. What's not to love about a room designed for one that has a locking door? And who can possibly argue with the reply "Not now, I'm on the toilet"? If things get too overwhelming, I just schedule myself a dentist appointment. There is nothing like a root canal to secure some guilt-free me time. One medicated hour in the chair with no disturbances can be pure bliss, and as a special bonus, I get to leave with a Vicodin prescription.

Constant proximity to my family is not a problem for now, but may become one in the very near future. I fear man smell the way some people fear snakes or spiders, and because I have five boys, my fears are not unfounded. An older boy named Oskar lives in our building; when he was going through puberty, I could literally smell him move past our floor in the elevator. My thirteen-year-old hasn't yet fallen headlong into the fetid depths of puberty, but one stroll down the seventh-grade hallway gives me a hint of what I am in for, and it doesn't smell pretty. It is the putrid hormonal by-product of boys turning into men.

"Why do you all smell so bad?" I asked Peik after I was safely outside the building and once again able to breathe through my nose.

"You mean this?" He struck a superhero pose. "I busted in there, and with one flex the smell of man bounced off the walls."

"Put your man smell away already," I said, trying not to laugh at him.

In an attempt to ward off the inevitable, I have tried to stock up on odor-blocking body products, the way John Birch Society members fill their basements with canned food, but in my heart I know there isn't enough Old Spice High Endurance Long Lasting Stop Smelling Up My Damn House Deodorant Stick in the world. And really, what is more disgusting, the stench of newly minted manhood, or the stench of newly minted manhood with a side order of "Mountain Fresh"?

I've done the math. Assuming man smell lasts for only two years—and I trust it is temporary, because my husband doesn't stink—by the time all five of my boys have passed through the noisome years of puberty and I can take a deep breath in my own home, the year will be 2023.

Mini-men aren't the only thing with an off smell in this loft. Our apartment could double as a petting zoo. I have successfully denied the kids anything large that would really require care, like a dog or a cat, but the small animals keep making their way into our household. We have a goldfish named Bubble Bath who swims in a vase on the kitchen counter, completely ignored by whichever child asserted that he would "prove I can take care of a dog" by receiving the fish. It was a short stroll to the hamster request. Ours is an insomniac who spends his nights running on a wheel that squeaks, and his days attempting to chew his way out of his ten-gallon glass aquarium home. I have applied countless rounds of WD-40 to that little circus ride, but the urine-induced rust just doesn't seem to respond and the nightly squeaking continues. He is not a friendly creature—none of my five boys dares to handle him.

If Hamster is unfriendly, our rabbit can only be described as downright vicious. Princess started out as a "class rabbit," which makes her sound more appealing than she is. She came home for Christmas vacation one year and never left. Small wonder the teacher never put in a call of concern regarding Princess's whereabouts. Again, I have no idea what child conspired against me to get another mouth into the house, but none of them seem particularly interested in taking the kind of loving ownership necessary to overcome Princess's issues. I was not there for her formative years, so I don't know the root of her problems, but she has so much anger and is so aggressive that the killer rabbit from *Monty Python and the Holy Grail* is a Muppet in comparison. Princess roams free because we are afraid to come in direct physical contact with her. She has a cage where food, water, and a litter box are provided for her, but she enters only at her own discretion. Once while I was working on my computer, intent on my keyboard and semi-oblivious to my surroundings, I sensed something moving off to my left.

"Mmmm, Cocoa Puffs," Peik said.

We're out of Cocoa Puffs, I thought as I continued to click away on an assignment. And then it hit me. I turned in slow motion from my desk to see my son's mouth closed, jaw moving.

"NOOOOOO!" I yelled as I snapped out of my trance. But it was too late. Realizing what he had eaten, Peik started spitting and running through the house screaming. I suspect that child is off breakfast cereal for life.

My favorite pet is Frank, short for Frankentortoise, a five-

year-old red-footed tortoise who, like Princess but for entirely
favorable reasons, has free rein of the apartment and a "Don't
ask, don't tell" potty policy. Don't ask me where he does it, because I can't tell you. Though the children have offered his
poop to guests, luckily none has ever eaten tortoise turds.
Frank recognizes people; he especially loves Zoila, who is always happy to give him a handful of the real Cocoa Puffs that
Peik now refuses to eat.

We also have a very large, very noisy cage of tiny finches
in the front of the loft. Despite their distance from the bedrooms, I can hear them in the wee hours chirping in harmony
to Hamster's machinations at the very first hint of daylight. I
am surprised they have the intelligence to do so, because we
started with a pair, and those fecund little birdstards have
multiplied into what is undoubtedly the most inbred, genetically mutant tribe since the Kennedys. By rough count at least
forty birds have been created in the past twelve years. Cur-
rently there are twelve, which seems to be one too many because one of them is pecked at by his friends so often that his
neck is slowly becoming devoid of feathers—he looks like a
sad little man, flying slowly behind the flock as they swoop
from one end of the ten-foot-long antique bird cage to the
other in synchronized flight. They might eventually kill him.
This is what happens when you live in one room with too
many inhabitants. We could put him in his own cage, but he
would then likely die of loneliness. It's Manhattan survival in
miniature.

A FRIEND OF MINE ONCE TOLD ME THAT HER MOTHER HAD SCOLDED
her for "overscheduling" her two children. Here's the thing
about having children in Manhattan: there is no such thing as

overscheduling, and anyone who calls you out on it is jealous because their town doesn't offer the variety of after-school lessons and experiences our town does. If New York City is Disneyland for adults, then it is freaking Epcot Center, Disney World, and Space Mountain for kids. There is no end to the things a child can learn and experience here. Filmmaking? Kendo? Basketweaving? Rock climbing? Sculpture? Oboe? Interpretive dance? We have it all.

My kids don't have too many extracurricular things going on, because lessons tend to be expensive and add total chaos to my schedule, but I do make sure each child has a unique activity that corresponds to his talents. Peik has his music, Truman has fencing, Pierson has male modeling, and Larson has art.

One afternoon, Larson was working on a paint-a-tie-for-your-dad kit I had picked up for him at Jack's 99 Cents. Because Larson is surrounded by some of the most amazing art and architecture in the world, he has developed a great deal of personal style and artistic ability. He was distracted from the project, though, by a favorite SpongeBob episode on the television, so he didn't do his best work. He didn't seem to think Peter would mind, though, and presented the result to him just as we were headed out to the Tribeca Ball, a benefit for the New York Academy of Art. Peter stripped off his ancient Hermès tie and put Larson's on, much to our son's delight. A few hours later, at dinner, the grande dame of art herself, Eileen Guggenheim, leaned over to Peter from a table away.

"What artist painted your tie?" she said, barely touching a finger to it.

"An outsider who goes by the name of Larson," Peter said in all seriousness, though there was a glint in his eye.

"Ah," she replied, leaning back to her own table, but only

after giving him a knowing look, one that said she had heard of this new artist, and he was going to be a *big* success.

AT A COCKTAIL PARTY NOT LONG AGO, I STARTED CHATTING UP AN-other guest. She was a typical New York Upper East Side so-cialite, attractive, sleekly dressed, perfectly coiffed hair, in her mid-forties, with just a tad too much Botox as evidenced by her huge, motionless forehead. We ran through the custom-ary small talk about where we live in the city and what we do; I told her about my ridiculous living conditions, which led to comparing notes on children. I went on a bit about my six, their various activities, and basically how challenging it is to keep the kids all alive, which is clearly the main objective of any parent.

"Yes," she said, "I know how hard it is to keep your little ones out of harm's way. Why, just this past month I almost lost my baby, Lily." She paused to take an exaggerated breath.

"Go on," I encouraged, moved by this terrible admission and at the same time dying to know all.

"Well, it was just heartbreaking to have to spend Christ-mas in the intensive care ward when all the other darlings were at home, waiting for Santa."

"You poor thing." I opened my eyes wider in what I hoped looked like an invitation to say more.

"Yes. It was as close to tragic as I ever hope to come."

"I can imagine," I said, leaning forward. At this point I re-ally needed some specifics to find the right empathetic chord to strike—this is what people do: we share our own challenges to let another person know that we understand their pain. I was already flipping through my memory picture book, past the time that Cleo shoved pearls up her nose, straight to the time that Peik had emergency surgery for a septic knee. I found nothing quite as wrenching as spending Christmas in intensive care. "How did she get there?" I queried, very gently. Sometimes people don't like to talk about accidents or diseases, especially at fancy cocktail parties.

"Well, she was sitting right there." The woman pointed at an imaginary object. "On the counter at Bergdorf's, patiently waiting for Mommy to make a special purchase." I recalibrated my mental picture of Lily to reflect perhaps a pre-walking infant, something that sits up on a department store counter. "When just like that, some thoughtless person offered her a *treat,* can you imagine?"

"Um, no," I said, thinking: Well, it's not unheard-of to give a kid candy at Christmas.

"And then it happened!" she exclaimed in a hushed voice, nearly dropping her Sauvignon Blanc as she swept her other hand in front of her. "Lily jumped down off the counter to get the treat and broke her back!"

Now I did feel some real sympathy. A small child with a broken back is serious.

"Yes," she moaned. "Thank God she had on her Chanel booties, or God only knows what would have happened to her paws. Four days in the hospital. Can you imagine?"

"Oh," I said. "Her *paws.*"

"Yes, poor little Tiger Lily may never be able to have another pedicure, what with the damage to her nails."

"Tiger Lily? You're talking about a dog?" I said, unable to politely hide my disgust. A swirl of thoughts raced through my head: I've got to get back downtown; I want my ten minutes back; why does Karl Lagerfeld design dog shoes? This woman was a walking example of exactly why I won't have a dog in the city, especially not one that will fit in a purse—that

kind of dog will make you a crazy person before you are ready to be one. Once all my circuits are snapped and I'm wandering around with my latest gay boyfriend, wearing feather boas and too much jewelry, then and only then will I have a dog. If any of my children want a dog, they can move out and get one. I need to remain a safe distance from this particular banana peel.

ALL THAT SAID, FOR EVERY WOMAN IN NEW YORK WHO TREATS HER shih tzu like a child, there is a woman who treats her child like a shih tzu—prized, groomed, pampered, and coddled to within an inch of its life.

I was at a parents' meeting at school one morning, talking to one of the new moms—an attractive, petite, divorced woman around my age. She was telling me about her difficult relationship with her ex-husband. There was a distinct sound of bitterness in her voice, which didn't surprise me once I understood he had left her for a twenty-four-year-old.

"He really crossed a line last week," she said. "I'm going to have my lawyer work on getting his custody rights revoked. My case is ironclad—you cannot believe what he did."

"What did he do?" I had to ask. After all, I often have divorce fantasies that result in Peter getting sole custody of all the children, even Cleo, who has been out of the house for a good seven years already. Just for some peace and quiet. That's what my grounds for divorce would be: irreconcilable noises. I often tell Peter, "If I ever leave, *you get the boys.*" It's all in good fun, but I imagined that this mom's problems must have something to do with Ecstasy pills rolling out of the girlfriend's slack mouth, or her pole-dancing friends coming over for a weekend performance. Something juicy, or half naked at the very least.

"Well"—she sniffed, half angry, half distraught—"he packed their lunches with Cheetos, Go-Gurts, and bologna sandwiches on *white bread.*" She sat back, satisfied. My mouth fell open, so she continued. "Do you have any idea how dangerous high-fructose corn syrup is? It is in every single one of those products! And the cheese single must have been made out of milk from cows who have been given hormones and antibiotics. When the children are in my care, I poach Amish-raised, grass-fed, free-range chicken breasts and stuff them into whole-grain pitas with hydroponic tomatoes and micro-greens that we grow in our own kitchen. How could he possibly endanger them in this way? *And* undermine my attempts to keep them from being poisoned by the agribusinesses that are the cornerstones of the nation's obesity and diabetes epidemics?"

"It's a good question, I'm sure," I said. She probably took the look of shock on my face as kindred-spiritedness. I'm all for a nutritious diet, and I personally despise Go-Gurts, which are single-serving tubes of yogurt waiting to be set on a table and exploded by the force of a small boy's fist applied to one end. They are capable of nailing a victim at thirty feet and making in a mess that only *CSI: Miami* could begin to unravel. But as I sat there hearing about other dietary transgressions, I couldn't help thinking that perhaps it was this woman's husband who should be pursuing a custody change. Her reaction was maniacally disproportionate. Junk food is not child abuse. Not in anybody's book. I quickly made a mental note of this mom's name so that when she called for a play date I could demur. It's bad enough that my kids would starve at her house and never, ever forgive me for subjecting them to tofu. But even worse, here's what would happen if her kids came to my house:

They would have no sense of moderation when faced with the forbidden fruit roll-up. Like winter-starved animals, they would dedicate themselves to consuming the lifetime allotment of sugar they had so far been denied. They would rapidly learn to lie about what they had eaten, because they would twig to the reality that their mother was keeping them from the things they loved and craved. This craving would become so all-consuming that they would question your authority in all other areas. Soon they would be boosting Twinkies from the corner bodega, a behavior that can only lead to smoking pot and much higher crimes.

I've had children like this enter my apartment, walk directly to the cupboard, remove a family-size tub of Swiss Miss Cocoa, and stand there eating it with a spoon, then move on to conquer a jumbo box of frosted strawberry Pop-Tarts. Faced with three different brands of snack chips, these children run from the kitchen clutching Cool Ranch Doritos in one hand and French Onion Sun Chips in the other, only to be found an hour later in the corner of the boys' bedroom, curled in the fetal position amid the empty packages, unable to state their own names.

Sheltering children from every evil in the word as if they were precious pets does them a disservice; decision making is a skill, learned with practice from the time they are small. Put a cute little bow on young Fido's head if you must, and feed him his whole-wheat whole-meal whole-grain puppy diet. But then do me a favor and keep your lapdog out of my house; I don't need a Milk-Bone overdose on my conscience.

At some point my boys will go out into the world and have to decide for themselves what is right and wrong. One would hope that they will have ascertained by then that Krispy Kreme doughnuts are not really for breakfast and that there are serious repercussions if you leave the mother of your children for a twenty-four-year-old.

"There's only poop on one hand. Do I have to
wash them both?"

GINGER BITCH AND OTHER PARENTING FAUX PAS

ruman (texting): OM fucking G, mom.

Me (also texting): What's the matter?

T: A kid here at sk8 camp can't ollie but he got tapped as sk8r of the wk.

M: Maybe you didn't get tapped because of your filthy language.

T: Dude, sk8rs swear, it's part of the credo. A kid here called me a ginger bitch.

M: Tell him he's stupid. A bitch is a girl; you're a ginger bastard.

T: OMG mom!!!

M: Not technically, but grammatically is all I'm saying :o)

Truman was texting me from skateboard camp. Getting tapped is the equivalent of winning the best camper award. I started out with the best of maternal intentions, reminding him to clean up his language, and then I got off track. It happens to me a lot when it comes to my parenting.

I was recently cruising a mom website where women were invited to confess their worst sins of motherhood. One woman admitted—with the kind of guilt better associated with an appearance in night court—that she fed her baby purchased food from a jar. The horror. She said she had always meant to make the baby's food herself, but couldn't find the time. Tsk tsk. Another woman came forward with the shocker that she allowed her child to sleep in pajamas that were not government-approved as sleepwear. I don't even know how you might find out such a thing about your clothes. Yet another poor soul declared that she washed her baby's bottles in the dishwasher, even though she felt in her heart that the water temperature was not high enough to properly sterilize them. Well, bless me, Father, for I have sinned: say three Hail Marys and have a martini. These children were fed, clothed, and cleaned. What exactly is bad about any of that? And if these women are the measure of good mommying, then I'd better buy myself a new stick, a rosary, and a bottle of Tanqueray.

I could certainly beat myself up over my boys' use of colorful language, but there's only so much I can do about it without them rightly calling me a hypocrite. I try to encourage them to be more creative with their vocabularies, but the truth is, sometimes there is nothing as satisfying as a good healthy expletive. The way I see it, regardless of how many times I try to get them to stop, they are going to swear. Cursing is a lot like nose picking—it's going to happen, so why waste my time correcting the behavior? My effort is better spent teaching them the appropriate place for such things. Booger retrieval, masturbation: that's why God put doors on bathrooms, I tell them. Do what you have to do in the privacy of your toilet time, wash your hands thoroughly, and don't tell me a word about it. Likewise, do your swearing where you won't be overheard by an adult or a tattletale.

One time in the fourth grade, Cleo was sent to the office for calling a classmate gay. Mind you, she was not mistaken. Despite her youth, she seemed to have some understanding of the word. Back when the boy in question came to stay the weekend with us in the country, I had found him in the garage trying on women's clothing—specifically, a silver lamé gown, which I then shortened for him and let him take home. During his visit, he tripped on the stairs and tumbled down one or two to the bottom. He lay on the landing, wailing for fifteen minutes, a reaction that can only be described as drama, and that provided further evidence for Cleo's eventual assessment.

When I sat her down to give her the obligatory parental speech about not calling names, I got very off track. I explained how difficult it must be to suspect that you are gay, and how different you must feel from everyone else. I said that calling the boy gay and thereby pointing out his perceived differences in front of others was hurtful and could make his situation even more uncomfortable because she had vocalized his worst fear—not that he prefers boys to girls, or Judy Garland to Angelina Jolie, but, in short, that he is *different*. Kids don't want to be different, I told Cleo, they want to be the same. So she should reach out to him—maybe the two of them could find something in common that made him feel "normal." I used air quotes.

When my job was done, and Cleo had left the room, Peter looked at me like I was crazy.

"What was that all about?" he asked.

"What?" I said, proud of how I had handled things.

"That wasn't what you were supposed to tell her. 'Help make him feel normal'? How about 'Don't call people names'?"

I could see his point. Perhaps it wasn't the right occasion to teach Cleo about the self-esteem issues of gay boys. Especially boys who didn't know that they were gay, or even know what "gay" is. But it's never too early to teach a child tolerance, and so I felt my time was far from wasted.

Sometimes I think I do better with the little kids. Life is so much more clear-cut when you're four. Pierson came out of the bathroom with poop on his hand. As you can imagine, bathroom issues in a house with six males are endless.

"There's poop on your hands; go back in the bathroom and wash them."

"There's only poop one hand. Do I have to wash them both?"

In this case my message was clear and the solution was clear, on track, and nonnegotiable.

IN A WORLD THAT HAS BECOME SO POLITICALLY CORRECT THAT Santa Claus has to be careful whom he calls a ho, it's no surprise that even the lowly peanut has become a target. There is a suburban myth floating around about a Massachusetts school district that recently evacuated a school bus of ten-year-old passengers after a stray peanut was found on the floor. Not an unclaimed backpack that could contain a bomb, not a mysterious white powdered substance. A peanut.

Once your child enters the great world of pre-k education, you are suddenly introduced to the concept that a classmate might die right in front of him if he brings a peanut butter sandwich for lunch, or in some special cases, any item in the nut or seed family. Thank God soy-based meat alternatives aren't banned, because I don't even know what those are. I fully acknowledge that there are children who have life-threatening nut allergies and their parents must work to ensure their safety. I am not an anaphylaxis denier. But I have to wonder—where were these kids when I was growing up? Did they just fall dead under the cafeteria table, swept up with the dropped spaghetti? What is causing the rise of the killer peanut?

There are parents with legitimate concerns, but I can't help but believe that a few are needlessly jumping on the bandwagon. Every now and then I encounter a parent determined to have a child who is special in some way—any way—that keeps the child dependent. It's a kind of Munchausen's by peanut. Other kids are getting special attention, why not mine? I once knew a mother who had her son, Acheron, convinced that if he so much as looked at a peanut, he would instantaneously begin dying a torturous death by strangulation and suffocation. And, not to get off the subject, but who names their child Acheron? In Greek mythology, Acheron is the river bordering Hades. It is a branch of the river Styx, where the newly dead are ferried into hell. Basically, the kid's name predicts a lifetime of woe that ends in misery, and his mother was going to make damn sure the prophecy came true.

She dragged Acheron around to allergists, looking for the evil airborne particles that would cause his untimely end. After endless rounds of scratch testing and other tortures, none of the doctors could find anything that he was allergic to, but his mom decided that she didn't trust the science. Acheron was required to carry an Epi-pen around with him in a small backpack emblazoned with a red cross so he could save his own life in case of emergency—a challenge I find most eight-year-olds not exactly up for. She might as well have embroidered "Kick Me" on the little kit. Happily, no symptoms of death ever occurred, but Acheron lived in fear nonetheless—fear of peanuts *and* bullies.

One day Acheron's mom called me to complain that my son had brought homemade chocolate chip cookies to school to share with his classmates. Also, she went on to tell me, I was guilty of buying her child a soft-serve cone from the Mister Softee truck on the way home from school the day I helped her out by covering pickup. Apparently Acheron had told her that he felt compelled to eat these treats because my son was his friend. I was trying to figure out why this boy would confess to his mother what he had eaten. Then she told me it was irresponsible of me to send *homemade* food instead of *packaged* food that had a label her son could scan for evil ingredients. Hang on, I put in. Homemade cookies do not come out of my house. The cookies were made from purchased gourmet dough, and there was indeed a label on the container, and Alicia had checked it. I'm not out to kill your kid with my store-bought homemade nanny-baked cookies, I said. I then suggested that perhaps our children shouldn't play together anymore; I have no problem with your child, I told her, but the way you're torturing him is driving me nuts.

After a brief silence, the mom mumbled something between an apology and a plea for sympathy, asking me to reconsider, as my son was one of Acheron's very few friends—no surprise. By that time I was spooning a lump of peanut butter into my mouth and wondering what would become of this child.

Why did this woman feel the need to unnecessarily traumatize her child? Did the thought of him being in constant mortal danger give her a sense of purpose? I have no problem refraining from dipping into the Skippy if doing that will save the life of a child, but do I have to take prophylactic measures against allergies that don't exist? Ghost allergies? Ironically, science shows that exposure to peanuts in school-age children actually reduces the risk of allergies. Avoiding nuts out of fear becomes a self-fulfilling snack-time prophecy.

As if raising healthy children isn't time-consuming enough, how do these moms find the time or energy to deal with crises that don't even exist? Once we get them vaccinated, checked up, louse-free, de-pinkeyed, and straight-toothed, and have the occasional broken bone set, who has time for any more medical drama?

And why do these hypervigilant parents single out nuts? If the peanut is such a threat to the general population that schools "have peanut-free zones," why not insist on shrimp-free schools? While 3.3 million people are allergic to nuts, 6.9 million are at risk from treacherous crustaceans. Lightning causes 100 deaths per year, about as many as die from all food allergies combined. Should children be required to wear little helmets with lightning rods affixed to them?

Apparently adults need to be special these days, too. Peanut hysteria seems to be part of a wave of new serious conditions that went either unnamed or unacknowledged when I was growing up—conditions like lactose intolerance, formerly known as burping and farting; restless legs syndrome, formerly known as "Get up and take a walk"; or the grand-daddy of all illnesses that didn't previously exist, chronic fatigue syndrome, formerly known as motherhood.

Don't get me wrong; I'm hardly the perfect school mommy. In fact, I think I've given new meaning to No Child Left Behind. My worst mommy crimes tend to happen when I forget where all my kids are. My friend Libby has had to call me several times at 8:30 P.M. because I've forgotten to pick Truman up from an "afterschool" hangout. I've also gone to Beau's house to get Truman when he's actually at Mason's, and one time Peik went to spend the night at Gordon's and it took me a couple of days to figure out that he wasn't home. Of course Alicia knew where he was, but it didn't even occur to me to ask her. Even little Finn has made his escape from my Alcatraz by slipping unnoticed down the elevator and into the lobby before being stopped by a neighbor.

Luckily for me, my kids are very self-reliant around the apartment. They take this practice to the extreme when they are guests elsewhere—I've often been thanked at the late pickup time (when I've eventually remembered where that missing kid must be) for how gracious and helpful my son is, how he put his dishes in the sink or he played with the younger children while the mom took a shower, worked out, what have you. Still, as full as my house is, it probably wouldn't hurt for me to do a head count around six instead of at eight-thirty, when Nicole is lining them up for baths.

I NEVER UNDERSTAND THE MOTHERS WHO GET EXCITED JUST BEFORE summer break, as if getting to sleep for thirty extra minutes in the morning is worth having to take care of your own kids all day. Sure, camp helps, but there is no camp that can possibly accommodate all five of my boys. Besides, sleepaway camps don't take toddlers. Not for three straight months, anyway.

As September rolls around, I joyfully get the kids ready for school. I secure the necessary color-coded folders and three-ring binders. I stock up on loose-leaf paper and mechanical pencils. I fill out all the necessary forms and artfully forged vaccination records so that everything appears up-to-date. I dig out backpacks with operating zippers, and rotate summer clothes, providing easy access to back-to-school wardrobes. I line up nannies and mannies, reading tutors and homework helpers, because God knows New York City private school tuition is not enough to cover the actual cost of education. Armed with the appropriate pharmaceuticals, I can sit back and watch my carefully hatched plan spring into action: avoid the children during school hours at all costs.

This fall I made it exactly one month into classes before having to set foot on campus. Not an easy feat, but between my husband, the afternoon nanny, and my oldest coming and going on his own, I was able to rig it so that others did the dropoffs and pickups. Then Nicole fell sick and I had to pick up Pierson. I didn't know where his classroom was or who his teachers were. I spotted a familiar face, the father of one of my son's friends.

"Hi, Dan."

"Hi, Laura."

"How are things?"

"Fine."

"If I were to want to pick up a child in first grade, what floor would I be on?" I asked sheepishly.

"You don't know where Pierson's classroom is, do you?"

Busted.

There are mothers who wouldn't dream of missing a

moment of their child's educational experience. They hover around the door of their first grader's classroom and peek through the window at intervals to check for signs of separation anxiety, ready to leap in and assure their child that unconditional love is lurking nearby. I am not that type. Frankly, my six-year-old doesn't need me to be, as evidenced by the first time he walked into his classroom, comfortable and confident, looked around, and said, "Where the hell is my cubby?"

Here in the city we have an urban myth that families are forced to move out to the suburbs because their kids didn't get into private school—they run screaming to the quiet hamlets of New Jersey or Connecticut to seek a decent public school. Much like the Hermès bag waiting list, this is pure fiction: I have never in my fifteen years here met one person who has waited two years for a purse or moved out of the city because of a catastrophic preschool denial. I do know people who have moved out because they thought the public schools sucked and couldn't bear the thought of paying $32,000 for kindergarten, but never anyone who just walked away. Real New Yorkers don't give up that easy.

Jon and Kate and their eight little goslings claim they are able to raise their family with the strength and courage they receive from God. That may work in the suburbs of Pennsylvania, but here in the city it takes money to raise a gaggle. *Lots* of money. The reality is that New York is an extremely expensive place to live, but that doesn't mean those who make it here are necessarily rich—we may earn bigger salaries, but we also have bigger bills. It's simply a matter of scale, and our scale is incomprehensible when compared to the suburban lifestyle. What with having to pay to park our car in a garage a taxi fare away from our front doors, or pay the grocery store to deliver the food that we don't have the luxury of throwing into the back of the SUV, the little things add up nearly as fast as the big ones, like rent, or mortgages, or a Larsonterages. This is where couples eventually choose to game the system: keep the big-city paycheck, but live a few commuter rail stops away from the burn rate of Manhattan. In the end, though, this means one parent gives up a hard-won career, because once in the suburbs you must spend quality time becoming part of a community—volunteering at the school library, coaching Little League, organizing bake sales. In the city we use our second incomes to pay people to do that crap for us. I've never once in fifteen years baked a cupcake for a class-room birthday. Why would I, when Cupcake Café can do it better, cheaper, and faster? And if I'm going to stay in the city, I'm going to buy the best education I can afford, just as I would go to Memorial Sloan-Kettering Cancer Center if I found a lump, and not some rinky-dink hospital that doesn't have "cancer" right there in the name.

The private school application process is daunting, but I'd say the panic is caused by parents: if every family would sim-ply apply only to the three schools they are most interested in, instead of applying to ten schools and clogging up the admis-sions process, everyone would get what they want in some measure. I have even seen families turn down a school accep-tance because they decided they couldn't afford it. Did they think a winning lottery ticket was in their future? Was Aunt Selma going to die and mention little Johnny in her will? Was the school going to hold an unprecedented tuition clearance sale? Why are these people clogging up the system? I actually don't know anyone who didn't get their kid into private school if that's what they wanted. There are enough spaces to go around.

Believe me, if the process were easy, and people could just

walk into the hallowed halls of the school of their choice, check in hand, New York parents would not be interested. We expect to have to win.

"EXECUTE YOUR ENEMIES. LEAVE NO SURVIVORS," A MENACING voice intoned over the cacophony of warfare coming out of the TV connected to the Xbox.

"What was that?" I exclaimed, turning from my desk toward my son. Peik was hunched over the controls, oblivious to the world. I do allow them to play war games, but even I have my limits. I draw the line at executions.

"Turn it *off!*" I yelled, getting up from my chair.

"I can't," he claimed, not looking at me. "I am in the middle of a mission, and I can't save now." I have heard this excuse before.

"I said, turn it off." Peik casually reached over to the remote and pressed the mute button without losing the spray of bullets coming from his avatar's AK-47.

"Turning the sound off is not turning the *game* off!" I shouted. "Turn it off now." Only when I made a move for the power button, and he feared he would lose everything, did Peik pause the game and come over to me.

"But, Mom, you know that I have to get to mission nine or I won't be able to upgrade to an M-16. With an M-16, I could blow my enemies to hell."

"Halfway to hell with an AK-47 will do just fine." I looked him in the eye, unblinking.

"Okay, okay," he said, throwing his hands up in the air and retreating to the boys' room, no doubt to log on to yet another game on the Internet.

With five boys comes violence; there's just no way around

it. They make guns out of jumbo crayons or potatoes, or just their damn fingers. They play violent games of their own devising, so I can't just expect my kids not to indulge at all. For quite a while I tried to keep up with all the videos, DVDs, games, iTunes downloads, and other media streaming into my kids' heads. This was a full-time job. Eventually I decided that I would check in every once in awhile, but that I wasn't going to let it drive me crazy. Denying the boys these outlets just makes them forbidden fruit. I would rather they learn to make choices and set limits for themselves. There are elements of pop culture that are violent and cruel, fast paced and sexual, but it's their culture; who am I to deny it to them? My mom let me watch *Love, American Style.*

SCIENTISTS AT RUTGERS UNIVERSITY HAVE RECENTLY ISOLATED THE gene that causes overprotective motherhood. I kid you not. Genetically engineered mice without the gene, known as oncoprotein 18, were slow to retrieve roaming pups and showed no concern when the pups interacted with unknown peers. By contrast, mice with the gene, or "helicopter mice," made sure that their pups ate lunch in a peanut-free school and called them on their cell phones three times a day.

I am certain that I was born without this gene. Now I understand why I let my kids ride bikes without helmets and eat snacks replete with preservatives and artificial colors while other mothers are making their teenagers use safety scissors. I have a genetic predisposition to laissez-faire parenting. The fact that I buy my children trampolines, go-carts, and motorcycles so they stay out of my way on weekends is not my fault. I have a disease.

It has nothing to do with the fact that I have six children

aged twenty years to twenty months and couldn't possibly care for them and remain sane without a team of nannies, mannies, tutors, therapists, and cleaning ladies. I am not lazy; I have the biochemical markers of a bad mommy. My mother passed on this genetic propensity to me. She allowed my brother and me to roam the neighborhood unsupervised with a gang of kids until the streetlights came on. She never stopped us when we chased the mosquito man's truck as it blew a cloud of DDT into our smiling faces. We were allowed to ride in the back of a station wagon without seats, much less seat belts. And we watched cartoons! Violent cartoons in which coyotes dropped anvils from red stone desert cliffs on passing roadrunners.

And to think for all these years I thought alcoholics were just undisciplined whiners who wouldn't take responsibility for their own actions. I totally get it now. Being a bad parent is a hereditary trait, no different from my green eyes or my dyed red hair. It's part of my DNA and has been passed down to me from generations of mothers who let their children fall behind in their immunizations, eat frozen dinners, and languish, forgotten, on playdates.

The truth is, my children are a bit *Lord of the Flies*. Given the chance, they do tend to run around like savages, half naked and covered in mud. I like it that way. I choose not to expend outrageous amounts of energy trying to get them to sit still when they will find a way to drive me nuts anyway. I find them funny. I don't want a bunch of buttoned-up, beaten-down miniature adults. My parenting style may be very different, but is it any less valid? I'll do my thing and you do yours.

Usually, though, I think it best to seek out friends who have similar parenting styles. Because that's all this really is, in the end: a matter of style. Every parent does the job a little differently, and I consider myself blessed when I stumble on people who can enjoy our chaos for what it is.

We recently had a couple over with their children, a "play-date" if you must, and there were seven kids buzzing around the apartment. These people were new acquaintances of ours. We hadn't been forced by proximity or similar-aged children into spending time with them, but instead had chosen to do so because of their appeal as adults. They had brought a lovely bottle of champagne, which we drank, and for a few hours we sat around and chatted and got to know one another better. Swirling around us was a virtual hurricane of activity. Balls were flying, swings were swinging, action figures were acting. Computers all over the house were pumping out iTunes, or the drone of World of Warcraft as keyboards went *tick, tick, tick.* The smaller children would occasionally look over at the television to pick up a clue from Blue, while the projector beamed wrestling matches from *Nacho Libre* up on the wall. One of my children decided to serve cheese and crackers to our guests, especially the lady, and insisted on preparing the delicacies with his grimy little hands. There was a potty inci-dent—there always is—and my four-year-old came shooting through the room in full Superman regalia, right down to the floor-length cape and bright red boots. At one point we had to separate my youngest boy from her youngest girl so as to terminate some tribal mating ritual known only to toddlers.

This all might sound a bit annoying, but my guests were not affected by it in any way. They knew how to laugh and seemed to be enjoying our combined cluster of boisterous children. I like these people. Mind you, there were seven kids between the ages of twenty months and twelve years barreling through our loft, but no one ever had to yell at anyone or level a time-out or complain about any injustice. (Well, who would dare, with Superman himself in the room?) For the most part the adults were being adults and the children were being children. The evening was very old-fashioned, really. It reminded me of the times my parents would visit with relatives or neighbors: my brother and I would run off and play with other kids' toys in other kids' rooms, knowing our parents were somewhere in the house, having adult time, which was boring. I spoke with one of my cousins the other day, and he said to me, "Laura, I still remember when you were eight and you would put on your Wonder Woman costume and run around the house like a crazy person, cape flowing out behind you. Do you remember that?"

Yes, I remember that. I still don the occasional costume.

In my house, things haven't really changed that much since the days of *Please Don't Eat the Daisies,* when the kids ran wild as the adults orbited around them, looking smart in their tea dresses and dapper suits. Jean Kerr didn't spend too much time worrying about how to raise her children; she mostly just got out of their way and then wrote about them so she could have a mental room of her own. I think maybe Nora Ephron nailed it in *I Feel Bad About My Neck,* when she wrote about how parenting as we know it is a modern phenomenon. There used to just be parents, now there is *parenting.* Somewhere between June Cleaver and Bree Van de Kamp there must be an explanation for how we got to a place where toddlers eat sushi.

"I say dress up every day. You never know when you
are going to meet your next husband."

FABULOUSLY GLAMOROUS

I WANT TO BE AUNTIE MAME WHEN I GROW UP. I WANT TO have an apartment with a sweeping staircase that I can descend daily, to be greeted by my dedicated staff and adoring assistants. I want to act as if money means nothing to me, because I am above concern with such things. I want to don glamorous cocktail dresses at five, and drip with jewels. I want to age gracefully, live without regret, and take full advantage of every opportunity that comes my way. I want to position myself in history as a gay icon, and that takes style.

Thanks to certain considerate movie directors, I have a very clear how-to guide. I have a ways to go—particularly in the "sweeping staircase" and "adoring assistant" departments—not to mention that Mame had one polite boy and I have five of the insane variety. Still, this clear picture is helpful in setting the standard for my personal style. Would Mame wear wrinkled capris and an ill-fitting T-shirt to her nephew Patrick's kindergarten performance at school? Would Mame show up at a black-tie affair in some plain-Jane dress and fade into the woodwork? Would Mame put her heirloom diamond cuff in a safety deposit box to languish, unused? Would she, at the lowest financial moment of her life, just give up on style and not dig to the bottom of her resourceful little soul to make sure she turned heads when she entered the room? Hell, no, and neither would I.

Style is not about money. It's about making a conscious decision to present yourself to the world in a particular manner. Does my style say my kids have taken over my life and I haven't had sex in decades? Or does it say I'm fabulous, and these boys are going to have a hell of a time finding a girl like dear old Mom? Style is about having a clear understanding of who you are and what you want out of life. It's about trusting your instincts and conveying your personal message. Style knows no age or size. It's easy to dismiss those with great style by saying "If I had a ton of money, I would have great style, too." I beg to differ. Gabrielle Chanel, an orphaned and penniless girl in France at the turn of the twentieth century, didn't let the poorhouse atmosphere stop her from becoming Coco. In fact, it may have helped. At this point in my life, I have more than I ever dreamed of, but it hasn't always been this way. Back when I was a struggling single working mother, I still dressed with great style. I feel lucky that I had to do more with less. It taught me a valuable lesson: money is by far the most overused accessory. You actually need very little to have great style.

I have too many kids and too little time, but I still manage to maintain a level of style. I dress up every day. It keeps me from getting sucked under. When you are forty-five years old and have six children, it's a slippery slope to sweat pants and a minivan. Dressing well actually takes very little effort, but it makes a huge difference in the way I feel and the way others feel about me. It is just as easy to pull on a simple dress or tailored trousers as it is to pull on a pair of tatty mom jeans. I have worked out a simple system that makes it easy to dress nicely every day and takes just a small amount of extra time. Think of it as developing a uniform.

First, you need to find the cinematic version of yourself. I don't expect the full frontal glamour of Auntie Mame to be for everyone; it takes a lot of guts to leave the house with your neckline plunging to your waist. I recommend instead that you find your own icon of cinematic style. How about the understated chic of Audrey Hepburn as Holly Golightly in *Breakfast at Tiffany's*? If you are looking for casual elegance, take a page from Katharine Hepburn's fabulous oeuvre and dress like you're vacationing *On Golden Pond*. Catherine Deneuve is the ultimate in retro sophistication in *Belle de Jour*, though I can't recommend her career choice. How about the menswear look of Diane Keaton in *Annie Hall*? I love the smart sexiness of Rene Russo in *The Thomas Crown Affair* and the theatricality of Jennifer Hudson as Effie White in *Dreamgirls*. Once you've chosen your fashion film, take your cues from your leading lady. Most movies will show your character dressing for all occasions, and don't forget to watch for hairstyles and accessories.

Once your personal vision is clear, seek out a few quality pieces that convey your vision and flatter your body type. These are the key wardrobe essentials, the basics of your uniform. The first thing to find is a simple, versatile dress that you can transform with accessories. Next on your list is a perfectly fitting pair of trousers and the type of skirt that works best on your body type. Add a great tailored jacket and a couple of nice blouses. It's that easy; these are the workhorses of any wardrobe, so this is where you want to go for quality over quantity. The clothes should fit you perfectly; have them tailored if necessary. These pieces don't need to be a matched set, but they should blend, so you can mix them together. If your simple dress is a bohemian print, think about a solid jacket with some handcrafted detail, so it has the same feeling as the dress and they can be worn together. Just fill in with some seasonal T-shirts, sweaters, and the occasional inexpensive trendy item, and I promise this wardrobe will take you anywhere in the world.

Now that your garment rack is looking purposeful, it is time to consider your shoe wardrobe. Personally, I believe the shoes make the outfit. A little black dress with a pair of sexy stilettos will get you through the cocktail hour looking sharp. That same dress worn with flat sandals or boots is perfect for daytime. Put on a serious shoe, like a feminine loafer, throw that aforementioned jacket over your shoulder, and the business world is yours. See how easy this game is? With a great evening shoe (supersexy required), a casual shoe (I don't mean sneakers), and an "I mean business shoe," your shoe wardrobe needs are covered.

The final category on your list of essentials is bags. This is another context where I can't overstress how important quality is. All you really need is a classic evening bag and a couple of day bags that give you color and size options. These should be thoughtful and careful purchases: your bag, like your shoes, can transform your basic clothing and help your personality come through. Consider what you are trying to say with your style, and make sure your bag says it.

Do not panic; I am not saying that once this concise list is complete you never get to shop again. I do not love shopping, but if you do, think of it as upgrading this master list of items. But beware. If you just keep adding, instead of upgrading these key pieces, your closet will become overwhelming, and dressing will become a chore. Keep it simple; make it easy.

DO NOT BELIEVE FOR ONE MOMENT THAT I OWN ONLY THREE PAIRS of shoes. Rules are, after all, meant to be broken, and shoes are a particular passion of mine. I collect shoes the way some people collect art; and while great style does not require great funds, I would be remiss if I led you to believe my shoes are inexpensive. Because I save so much money sewing my own clothes, I feel I get to spend more on shoes. In my defense, I still wear the first pair of Manolos I ever bought. After thirteen years of wear, they have been refurbished many times, but that pair of shoes long ago earned their keep.

My shoes are not neatly tucked away in a closet, nor are they relegated to dusty boxes affixed with Polaroids of what's inside. No, my shoes have pride of place in the middle of our loft, shelved like books where I can see them and be reminded of walking down the banks of the Seine in this pair, leaving the hospital with Larson in that pair. They are my little soldiers, standing at attention, waiting to go for a spin or to show themselves off to guests. I won't say that they make me happier than my children, but I won't say that they don't, either.

If there were a fire in my apartment, and I only had time

to grab one pair of shoes, I know exactly which pair it would be. Much as I have a favorite child, I have a favorite pair of shoes: my russet-colored alligator Manolo pumps. They have a three-and-a-half-inch heel, the ideal height for me, and they are the most glorious color. They match my hair, so no matter what color my black dress is, these shoes always work. The cut is low and sexy, dipping down the sides and front, revealing just the right amount of toe cleavage. They are my most expensive shoes, but that is merely a coincidence. The way these shoes make me feel when I slip them on is priceless.

I have four bags. Unbelievable, isn't it? I have only four bags, but they are so delicious I can pass by the purse selection of any department store without the slightest temptation to be unfaithful. Each bag represents a time, place, or event in my life. Whether the moment is one of amazing good fortune or scrappy ingenuity, a reward for a job well done, or the celebration of an event, my bags mark the passing of time. These intimate friends go with me everywhere; they inhabit my personal space. They know my secrets and can be trusted to keep them. I feel about these bags the way a person in L.A. must feel about his or her car. My bags are the loyal friends that provide me with the things I need all day, tucked away in their little compartments, ready for the asking.

Big things come in big packages, but sheer joy comes in small ones. When I was helping my husband sort through his recently deceased mother's storage space, I found my first—and smallest—bag. We had come across a garment box of old clothing, the kind with its own hanging rod. I was quite pregnant at the time and not all that interested in viewing Mrs. Shelton's size-way-smaller-than-me clothes when a tiny flash of light from the depths of the box caught my eye. I took a quick look around the room to make sure my sister-in-law was pointed in another direction and reached in, blindly letting my hand fall onto the most perfect, hard, rough-surfaced rectangle known to the bag world. I pulled it into the bare fluorescent light of the room and it was like walking into Studio 54. Shots of glimmering light spun around the place as I turned the treasure over in my hand. Yes, it was encrusted with crystals; yes, it was small enough to fit into my palm; and yes yes yes when I slid the clasp over and up it opened like Venus on the half shell to expose the tiny little gold plate with the words "Judith" and "Leiber" embossed thereon. In marvelous addition, nestled in the rich black velvet were a delicate silver comb with a tassel, a silver metallic-leather change purse, and a smile-width mirror. Drop in a lipstick and a twenty and the possibilities would be endless. I caught a glimpse of my belly in the mirror and came back to my senses long enough to give up an antique end table in order to make the minaudière (the word alone!) all mine. I cannot count the weddings this darling has been to, the awards ceremonies, the black-tie fund-raisers, I can't count the times it has spun around a dance floor. Was the table worth a lot more money? It never crosses my mind; the bag has been a lot more fun.

When Peik was born, I decided I needed a Birkin bag to go with him. Have you seen diaper bags? They come in the most hideous patterns and sizes. Or at least they did fourteen years ago, before smart designers like Kate Spade got into the game. There was no way I was going down that ugly road. A diaper bag is fine if you're throwing it in the back of a minivan where no one's going to see it, but I was not going to walk the streets of New York pushing a stroller with one of those monstrosities banging against my leg. An Hermès Birkin would serve the same purpose, I figured; it was roomy enough to fit Peik in a pinch, besides the diapers and wipes and all that stuff you need to keep a baby clean, dry, and happy. Why not make Mommy happy, too? I couldn't afford a new Birkin, so I started stalking the upscale thrift shops in New York City. I would stop by regularly and get to know the salespeople. If I were looking today, I would head for the Web, but this was the dawn of the Internet revolution. I left my name and phone number at every store, hoping if a Birkin came in they would give me first crack at it. One day I got the call: a forty centimeter, camel colored, with gold hardware. Gently used. Perfection. That bag has seen me through fifteen years and four more babies; most recently, this past weekend, it took on the contents of Pierson's Big Gulp blue Icee and didn't complain in the least. It seemed almost happy to help. That's a real friend.

My second Hermès bag was purchased during a trip to Paris with my husband. Brand-new, from the store on the Faubourg Saint Honoré. That was a real thrill. The bag came with all the accoutrements: a big orange box, brown ribbon, scads of tissue, a rain cover, and an orange flannel dust cover. I chose a sleek black Kelly bag in box calf. The Kelly bag is named for Grace Kelly, who carried one to cover her pregnancy; I looked like royalty myself sporting that bag around Paris. I love the bag's prim and proper shape, and the way it makes me feel always follows suit.

It was many years later that I received my third Hermès bag. Because I was the owner of classics in brown and black, I could afford to go a bit wild with this one. As a gift from Peter on the birth of my sixth child, I received an orange Haute à Courier with silver hardware. Similar to a Birkin, but with slightly different proportions, this bag is for fun. To me, it is the little red sports car of purses.

—

THIS SHOULD BE THE FIRST COMMANDMENT IN THE FASHION BIBLE: Thou Shalt Have a Little Black Dress. We have Coco to thank for that genius stroke as well. I came across my version in what was perhaps my most penniless time, just after my divorce and a few years after I had moved with my daughter to New York City. I was cruising the sale racks of T. J. Maxx, which is like saying I was walking around the pound looking for a Norwegian Lundehund, and there it was: an ankle-length Donna Karan with empire waist and scoop neck, for $14.95. It wasn't much to look at on the rack, but I'd been refashioning bargain clothes since I was ten and knew in an instant that if I took the hem up over the knee the dress would be exquisite on me. I've always had that knack, I guess, and mainly have my mom to thank—she was a sewing teacher and I learned everything I know at her elbow, the way some kids learn to bake cookies.

I was wearing that little black dress the night I met Peter, and then again on our first date. I've worn it between pregnancies, during pregnancies, and after pregnancies; I even rolled it out (with some lengthening) on the runway when I introduced my line of evening wear in Bryant Park, in front of the cameras, six months pregnant with Finn. I won't be surprised if they decide to bury me in that dress when I'm old and small and gray.

My passion for fashion may seem excessive, but remember: I live in a house full of destructive boys. My personal luxuries are the only things I can protect, the only things that don't get destroyed. Now is not the time for me to enjoy a porcelain collection, or nice furniture; and I really think Mame would approve.

If you think fashion is a venture for the intellectually inferior, I challenge you to give it a try. Dressing better will make you feel better. Who can deny the psychological lift of a new hairstyle or a well-cut dress? How about the feeling of "I'm worth it" that comes from a luxurious cashmere sweater, or the confidence you feel at work when you appear taller, slimmer, and more powerful in a great pair of heels? What we wear sends an unspoken message. It shows that you have taken the time to treat yourself well, and that others should, too. I say dress up every day; you never know when you're going to meet your next husband. Be exuberant, celebrate occasions large and small in how you dress, and remember, everyone appreciates glamour.

"I will proudly walk into my fifties with my ass
held high, thanks to my power panties."

THE LAURA BENNETT DIET™

A FEW YEARS AGO I WAS AT A SAMPLE SALE for one of my favorite designers. Most women I know dread communal dressing rooms more than they do the gynecologist, with their impersonal drapes, bad lighting, crowded mirrors, and female security guards watching your every half-naked move. The friend who was with me that day has been known to try clothes on over her jeans to avoid exposure. Me, I grabbed about a dozen garments for myself, handed her a dress I knew would work for her, and pointed her to the back of the room.

"I am not getting undressed," she said.

"You have to," I replied, grabbing another dress on our way. The room was packed, as feared, but I didn't care. I shepherded Rachel to a slightly more protected corner and we quickly peeled off our clothes.

"What are you wearing?" she exclaimed, looking over at me while trying to keep her thonged backside to the wall. "A girdle?"

"It's not a girdle, it's a power slip. And instead of worrying about what it's called, you should be asking me where to get one."

"But you don't need one of those—you look great."

"I look great because I have one of these. Trust me, it's the best diet out there." There is nothing like the instant gratification of looking ten pounds lighter and twenty years smoother when you pull on a pair of Lycra™-infused bike shorts.

And now you know the cornerstone of my diet. There have been the most amazing, life-altering advances in technology over the past decade—the BlackBerry, Google, iPods. How did I ever research papers as a college student? Keep up with distant family members? Buy books? Friend my third-grade crush? I won't do that last, but I could. I simply cannot remember life before broadband. These are all marvelous changes, but they don't hold a liquid crystal display to the introduction of high-tech fabrics. A glorious cocktail of Microfiber, Lycra, Spandex, and Elastine instantly transforms my butt. I love my shapewear. Perhaps I exaggerate the degree to which I loathe my lowest asset, but I know very, very few women over the age of thirty who don't have some body flaw here or there that wouldn't benefit from a firm foundation. Cinch the waist, tighten the tummy, raise the rear: there is a shape shifter for every task. Women wear bras in order to lift and separate; why not wear a bra for your butt?

Speaking of the latter, I do not envy a dating woman who has to remove a pair of nuclear-powered knickers for an impromptu romp. There really is no sexy way to extract oneself. As Bridget Jones found out the hard way, those events need to be carefully planned and prepared. Happily, I'm at a stage in my life where I dress to please myself. Besides, a good girdle might be all that stands between me and baby number seven.

"Six kids! You don't look like you have six kids."

I have to wonder what people think a woman with six kids looks like. I suspect they mean, "You don't look fat enough to have six kids." News flash: having babies does not make you fat. If having babies made you fat, I would be huge. Beyond huge. Taking in more calories than you burn off makes you fat. I think women get lazy, then blame babies for the demise of their figures. I blame a lot of my problems on my kids—the fact that I have little free time, the fact that I am nearly deaf, the fact that someone came into my bed in the middle of the night and peed—but not the fact that I have a big butt.

I do have to give some credit to genetics. It's easy to hide five pounds here or there on a five-foot-nine-inch frame. I have hardly won the genetic lottery, though, and I do contribute to staying in shape.

I am not much of an eater. And it's not that I have food issues or a "disorder"; I simply don't get a big kick out of great food. I'm what most people call a grazer. This does not complicate my marriage in any way, as Peter is not much of an eater himself. Every three days or so, he helps himself to a huge platter of fries and a bacon cheeseburger, and I rarely see him eat anything else. Because I don't often sit down for a full, satisfying repast, I tend to snack my way through the day. A handful of Goldfish here, a tablespoon of Skippy there, and a half hour later you might see me squirreling a bunch of almonds into my pocket to nibble on as I turn a seam. I often have crackers and cheese for dinner. Luckily for the boys, Alicia and Nicole make sure they are provided with those things called meals.

I have a deep-seated aversion to diets. I get nervous if my eating is restricted. If I have to have an Oreo, I have to have it. I just try to keep myself from eating the entire pack. I have no idea how women follow those diets that list specifically every item you need to eat at every meal. And frankly, if I ate the amount of food that most of those diets recommend, my ass would be the size of a double-wide trailer. I suspect my distrust of restrictive dieting is rooted in my own childhood. My parents once decided to go on the Atkins diet with the kind of fervor that made the plan so wildly popular—you had a license to eat bacon and cheese at every meal! Vegans aside, what red-blooded American wouldn't be thrilled with those instructions? Even as a child, I didn't see how it could be healthy, but they did manage to lose weight—my mom as much as twenty pounds, which she gained back as soon as she ate a serving of green beans. The traumatizing part for me was their breath: the chemical reaction from all-protein all-the-time was so profound that it would knock me over if my parents said good morning. I knew it was the diet because they both suddenly had the exact same odor from hell. In fact, it was so bad I can still conjure the smell today; it transports me back to my childhood home in an instant. Proust had his madeleines, I have my bacon breath.

I stumbled upon another cornerstone of the Laura Bennett Diet, something much more satisfying than food. After thirty years of three packs a day, my husband wisely decided to quit smoking. He endured two weeks of cold turkey, but I sensed he was faltering and bought him some nicotine gum. Having never been a smoker myself, I didn't understand the draw of cigarettes, but then I tried a piece of his Cinnamon Surge 2-mg coated Nicorette. It was ambrosia. I suddenly realized that nicotine is the most amazing legal substance of the twentieth century. I was immediately, happily, and willingly hooked.

I credit nicotine gum with everything from keeping me thin to saving my marriage, but I admit it has its hazards. Not health hazards—at least, not any that I know about or want to acknowledge—but child hazards. Peter shares my affection for nicotine gum, and if he sits in any one place too long, at the computer or TV for example, he amasses a small pile of chewed pieces. I want to believe that he has every intention of disposing of these properly, but it doesn't always happen, at least not in a timely manner. Naturally all the nicotine has been depleted, so it's not as though the children are going to get a second-hand chew if they put it in their mouths, but still, it's annoying.

One Sunday morning I was taking a bath—my rather long weekly bath, during which I try to catch up on personal maintenance. I heard Finn crying somewhere in the house and called in vain for someone, anyone, to check on him. There were at least six other people in the house who could have checked, after all. Receiving no reply, I left my legs half shaved and got out of the tub. I found Finn in the living room, standing on the coffee table, wearing a T-shirt and no diaper, his little genitals so completely encased in chewed nicotine gum that he looked like a baby hermaphrodite.

"Oh, my God," I said to Peter, "Look at what he has done!"

"Yeah, I saw that," he said.

In all fairness, had the problem been easier to deal with, like, say, the two hundredth spill of the day, Peter would have taken care of it, but this was, to say the least, a sticky situation. Well, thank God for the amazing citrus power of late-night-as-seen-on-TV cleaning products. It took half a bottle of Goo Gone to detach Finn's little testicles from the side of his leg.

Despite the downside of gum chewing, and its inevitable move into the realm of taboo, I will continue to chew nicotine gum because it is the closest I will ever get to Nirvana, and frankly, given all I go through with this circus of mine, I deserve a vice. When Peter falls asleep with a piece in his mouth, I will dutifully cut it out of his hair in the morning and thank God every day for my twelve-piece blister pack of heaven.

I WAS RECENTLY HIRED BY THE PHARMACEUTICAL GIANT GLAXO-SmithKline to design dresses for two women who had won a competition to lose weight by using a new diet pill the company had developed. I took part in the presentation of the dresses and a press conference. When the event was over, the executives invited me to dinner. I spent the meal buttonholing executives about the diet-pill potential of their other product, Nicorette.

"Oh, did you start chewing it to stop smoking?" one suit asked.

"No way," I said. "Smoking's for losers. I chew because nicotine keeps me sane." I went on to regale them with my thoughts on the product, about how when I put a piece of that gum in my mouth, and I feel that spicy taste running down my throat, a feeling of calm comes over me and all is right with the world. The fact that my mouth is busy chewing gum and not rabbiting popcorn or nibbling Triscuits is an added benefit in that it cuts some calories out of my day. I was willing to admit that I am so addicted that I get nervous when my supplies are low, so I have hidden gum all over the house and in random purses for emergency situations. I even have a friend who "holds" a blister pack for me, she is so worried about my mental state should I find myself without a fix.

"Really," I said, "I love it so much, I act like a pusher, constantly offering it to other people." By this time, I noticed that a few of the suits had left the table and the ones who remained were eyeing me skeptically, but with a small glint in their eyes. I have been waiting for the spokesmodel call ever since, and believe me, if you are out there, Mr. Nicotine Suit, I am *your girl.*

ANOTHER WAY I TRY TO CONTAIN MY BUTT IS BY RUNNING. IF I TRY TO tell you that I exercise for my health, don't believe me.

"Why don't you just join the YMCA?" Peter asked me one night as I peeled yet another layer of Lycra off my body.

"Old people go to the Y," I shot back.

"They have an indoor running track," he said.

Well, it was love at first sight. If I have to exercise, I would rather not suffer. Climate control is the way to go. I don't have to worry about freezing winter or steaming summer days. The track is small—an eighth of a mile—so I tend to feel like Hamster in his wheel, but after about fifteen minutes I zone into my endorphin high and don't really notice. I can spend a full hour just going in circles, passing the same old guy with his walker at least fifty times. If that doesn't make you feel good about yourself, what will? Sometimes, just to unwind, I will sit myself on an exercise bike alongside a woman with an oxygen mask, her personal video screen tuned to *The Price Is Right*. She's my inspiration. She's always there on Tuesdays and Thursdays, and I feel that she would be discouraged if I didn't show up as well.

Of course, dieting is partly an attempt to retain or regain a youthful appearance, which is why the majority of liposuction is performed on women over forty. One day as I was viewing my backside for the billionth time in the mirror, I flirted with the idea. I pictured my body facedown on an operating table. Naked. Concentric circles marking zones of imperfection drawn over my butt and thighs. Anonymous men in surgical gear discussing whether to have sushi or subs for lunch. Nurses quietly judging me for being so damn shallow, but happy to get a paycheck on the fifteenth and thirtieth of every month. A long rod slides violently in and out of my flesh, pulling lumps of bright yellow fat into a tube and then a plastic Ziploc bag, to be deposited God knows where on the planet. Then there are the weeks of healing, oozing sores connected to yet more tubes that you have to measure and empty every few hours. Gack.

I am not sure who the woman is who would opt for this over a twenty-five-dollar visit to the lingerie department at Macy's, but it's certainly not me. The idea of having my ass removed to a landfill is just too much to bear. I'm certainly not against cosmetic augmentation, as it is in keeping with my theory that you can make yourself feel good by making yourself look great. I dye my hair; I glue eyelashes onto my lids. I even once had Botox injected into my forehead. For this I went to a fancy uptown New York dermatologist frequented by many of my good friends. They all look terrific, I thought; this might be a good step. In the waiting room, reading *Town & Country* magazine, I began to take quick glances at the assorted women there. I began to get scared. Most of the women had an upper lip so filled with collagen that they could have half kissed their own noses just by ex- haling. Many foreheads were broad, expansive, smooth, im- mobile. I cocked an eyebrow just to feel my own scalp move in reassurance. A few women had a tell-tale puffiness around the eyes, an attempt at filling crow's feet quite apparent. Was it possible these women didn't know that they didn't look younger? That what they had accomplished with these vari- ous procedures was turning themselves into two-bit carica- tures of their mothers?

"Don't make me look like those women in the waiting room" was the first thing I said to the doctor.

"Those women are junkies. They go from doctor to doc- tor. It's their own fault they look that way," he assured me.

Well, the Botox looked fine, and for a few weeks I felt a tiny bit younger, maybe forty-three, but I never went back.

Then one night I was watching a Bravo reality show, one of the *Real Housewives* iterations. There was an attractive woman, divorced with two children, working hard to support her family. She wasn't just kicking back and relaxing on the proceeds of her alimony. By the third season, this character hooked up with a rich guy, and her looks totally went down- hill. She obviously now had access to money for procedures, and also had a newfound fear of the rich guy preferring a younger version of herself ere too long. What was once a pretty face morphed into a monster of alarming proportions. Her lips puffed up, her forehead grew, and she must have had cheek implants—how else could you explain the sudden re-semblance to Joan Rivers? Before she had money, she looked great. No, she didn't look twenty, but she rocked her forties.

I intentionally lie about my age. I actually tell people I am older than I am.

"Fifty! Wow, you look great for fifty!" I may not be able to look like a girl in my thirties, but I can kick some fifties ass.

I've decided to forgo injections and fillers because I fully intend to become a crazy old lady who wears too much makeup, piles on all of her jewelry at once, and prances around the house in an enormous wig and a feather boa, like a redheaded Carol Channing. By the time I am wizened and wrinkled, my gay icon status will be improved upon by my greatest gift to my fans: another version of me to emulate. Young Laura Bennett, *Project Runway* Laura Bennett, Pregnant Laura Bennett, Crazy Old Lady Laura Bennett—the character lines will give young cross-dressers so much more range to play with. And they, better than most, know a thing or two about the beauty of shape shifters.

For the moment, I don't fear aging at all. I will proudly walk into my fifties with my ass held high, thanks to my power panties.

Located next to a stinky dairy farm,
we call this place Dairy Air (pronounced derriere).

DAIRY AIR

I HATE IT WHEN MY KIDS WANT TO HELP. I KNOW HELPING is how they learn, but I just don't have the time or patience. Any task my kids assist with takes twice as long and yields four times the mess. I remember from my childhood a Duncan Hines commercial where the pretty apron-wearing mother prepares the cake mix with her three smiling children in a sparkling white kitchen, but in my house it never goes down that way. When Pierson insists on stirring the pancake batter, it ends up lumpy and all over the counter. If Truman wants to deliver a morning cup of coffee to his father, there is invariably a trail of joe leading from the kitchen to Peter's morning perch at the computer. Everything is just so much cleaner if I do it myself.

Driving home from the country the other night, we stopped for gas an hour outside of Manhattan, as is our habit. The best way to enjoy living in New York City is to run screaming from it every Friday. The downside is the effort required to transport five boys three hours in one car without incident. Necessity demands a midway break. We stop to fill the tank and let anyone who is still awake buy junk food from the gas station mini-mart. Pumping gas holds a phallic fascination for my boys, and Peter wasn't there to say no, so they immediately started begging me to let them wield the nozzle.

"Wait in the car; just let me do it myself," I said, but it was too late. The doors flew open and three of them escaped. Once a child is out of a five-point-harness car seat, there is little I can do to stem the riptide of testosterone. A scuffle ensued at the pump, because Pierson thought he should be the one in charge, and by the time I swiped my card and chose the octane level, Truman had won the battle with his brothers and was filling the tank. Truman has pumped gas before and he seemed to have it under control so I stepped aside, resisting any arguments from Pierson and Larson about how the scenario was *unfair.*

When the pump detected that the tank was full, the nozzle clicked and Truman, on cue, pulled it out of the car. Somehow forgetting his previous expertise, he failed to let go of the lever that stops the gas. Flammable liquid shot everywhere at full speed. He pointed the nozzle up, as if to use gravity to stop the deluge, but that only caused a gasoline fountain. Larson, Pierson, and I were screaming at him to let go when gas splashed into his eyes, and he finally dropped the hose—

which thankfully released the lever and stopped the river of gas. Pierson, who had been right up in Truman's grille vying for the pump, was soaked with gas and standing in a puddle of it. He looked down at his saturated clothes.

"I'm gonna blow!" he yelled over and over, taking off running in hysterical circles. The poor kid had recently watched the scene in *Zoolander* where the male models have a gasoline fight to the tune of "Wake Me Up Before You Go-Go" by Wham! on their way to buy orange mocha frappuccinos, then one of them lights a cigarette and sends everyone up in flames.

"Mom, I'm gonna blow!" he kept repeating. Peik, previously too lazy to leave the van, leaped out of the car and added to the mayhem by running around the gas station parking lot screaming, "I've got a match!" This sent Pierson into even greater hysteria. Meanwhile I did what I could to get us back on the road, picking up the hose and putting it in the machine while trying to avoid the puddles and not get gasoline on my Manolos.

"Screw the cap on," I directed Truman, trying not to yell at him in front of the gathering crowd. "Can you manage that?"

"But, Mom, really, it should be impossible to pull the pump out of the car while the gas is flowing," Truman insisted. "It *must* have malfunctioned."

"No, you dipwad," Peik said, taking a break from scaring the hell out of his little brother in order to debase this one. "How would you be able to fill a gas can, genius?"

Pierson had to be stripped of his soaked clothing. Larson, who was dressed as good Spider-Man, offered his bad alter ego Spider-Man costume, which he naturally had with him in case of emergency. It had built-in chest muscles and was so small it gave Pierson a wedgie and came up to his shins, but he was happy to put aside sartorial grievances in order to save himself from immolation. I threw his gas-soaked clothes in a garbage can.

"The show is over, folks," Peik announced to the parking lot crowd as we boarded the van and drove away. Once we were safely back on the road, we really gave it to Truman, who was embarrassed and angry that we were laughing at him for potentially turning our van into a suicide bomb.

After retaliating with a stream of unprintable curse words, most of which started with "mother," Truman declared, "When I grow up, I am going to be rich and you'll all be sorry!"

"What does that have to do with dousing your brother with gasoline?" Peik calmly asked, as I rolled down the window to ease my burning eyes. "This car freaking reeks."

"I like the smell," said Larson.

"Oh, great, a future stoner," Peik predicted.

The next time one of my kids offers to help me, I'm the one who's gonna blow.

WHEN I MET PETER, HE ALREADY OWNED A COUNTRY HOUSE, THE UL- timate luxury for a New Yorker. Being able to get out of the city makes me better able to appreciate living here. Because Peter was unmarried, the raised ranch was, unsurprisingly, a bachelor pad. A one-bedroom house works fine for a single man, or even a couple who get along well, but with our baby habit came a need for more space. The ranch house was also perched on a cliff, and Peter didn't have the stomach to look out the window and see an infant crawling toward a twenty-foot drop or a toddler scaling a rock wall. The roads were like-wise steep, and it wasn't unusual for Cleo to career down a hill at thirty miles an hour on her bicycle. We sold the house and drove north until we found something that met our needs and that we could afford. Proximity to New York City determines a property's value. The farther you drive, the more affordable real estate becomes. A second home in the hour range signifies that you are in the big bucks. This is not a completely linear system, as there are pockets of prestige here and there. You have to be on the lookout for what Peter calls the valley of value, which I suspect is somewhere near Brigadoon.

I have found that city people frequently lie about how long it takes to get to their country house. This is especially true of the Hamptons, an exclusive enclave of towns at the eastern end of Long Island. "It takes us about an hour and a half to get there" is the typical brag. Sure, in a Formula One car with a radar detector.

Our house is in the three-hour range, ideal for avoiding self-inviting houseguests. Three hours in a totally trashed van with five boys and one Butch Ballerina in uncomfortably close quarters. Before we even leave the parking garage, the boys are fighting over which movie they will watch. We have two DVD players so we can show flicks for two age groups, but the warfare over seats is still heated. By the time we reach the West Side Highway, someone has vomited. This is usually a by-product of the fight over the seats, which causes one of them to cry, thereby triggering the postsobbing gag reflex. By the time we pay the toll to cross the bridge out of Manhattan, the snacks and drinks brought from home have been spilled. This causes a seismic shift in the seating, because someone now needs to find a dry spot. Things then settle down until we hit the hour-and-a-half mark, at which point we stop at the Red Rooster. This tiny little hamburger stand in Brewster, New York, has become a habit for us, so much so that, like a speech-impaired Pavlov's dog, as soon as Larson gets his seat belt on in Manhattan he starts reciting his order.

"Are we stopping at da Woosta? I want a cheeseburga, Coke, and cirka, cirka, cirka."

This order is repeated endlessly until we get there, and in case you don't speak Larson, "cirka" means an onion ring, and he literally wants only three of them.

Once we are back on the road, over the remaining hour and a half of the trip milk shakes are picked up by the lids, which pop off every time, soaking chicken strips in ice cream sauce; cardboard boats of French fries drizzled with ketchup end up upside down on the floor; and every single weekend, Blake finishes the exact same order of fried food, with a calorie count equivalent to the recommended daily intake for an entire Broadway cast, and then complains that he's fat. A few miles on, the burping and farting commence, at first by nature and then increasingly by competition. Usually, with maybe five miles to go, at least one of the creatures in the back needs Peter to pull over so it can pee. By the time we finally arrive at our house, I hate my kids. Only the ones who have fallen asleep and the ones smart enough to pretend they are asleep are spared my arrival wrath.

The house is a converted barn in the Berkshires of Massachusetts; we call it Dairy Air. Next door is a dairy farm, and if the wind is blowing in the right direction, our entire property smells like derrière. The cows are lined up in large open-air sheds, standing in their own filth and producing enough methane to power a third-world country or at least provide the farmer with cable television. We thought it would be good for the children to be near real nature; maybe we could even buy milk from the neighbors. Instead, Peik has developed a

Tourettian habit of emerging from the car half asleep on Friday nights muttering "This place smells like ass."

Living in a converted barn sounds very romantic. Barns can be quite beautiful, with their simply pegged beams and dramatic, soaring, cathedral-like spaces. But our barn is more a glorified shed, not a majestic stone-foundation classic nestled on a wealthy old gentleman farmer's estate. Even more sadly, our structure was "converted" in the 1960s, when dropped ceilings and wood paneling were all the rage. There are no theatrical spaces with exposed historic woodwork overhead. It's all very practical, and no doubt easier to heat, but it won't be appearing in any design magazines. We have a dizzying amount of mod wallpaper and samples of every faux-finish painting technique that has been in fashion since 1970—marbleizing, sponging, decoupage; you name it, you can find it in this house. In a further attempt to obliterate any of the barn's original qualities, a previous owner attached a covered colonial entry smack in the middle of the barn's exterior. The minute we signed the closing papers, I attached the faux-authentic structure to a truck and pulled the whole thing off, much to the horror of my visiting parents. The truth is, the beautiful barn structure is there, it's just buried under Sheetrock walls, linoleum, and shag carpet. A real estate listing would use the phrase "hidden potential." Even with two architectural degrees between us, like the shoemakers, Peter and I have never attempted to give our children a better place to put their feet. We no longer have the energy or the resources to do anything about this mess. Besides, why put your money into something that five boys are going to destroy?

The basement floods on a regular basis, the roof has a series of suspicious peaks and valleys, the chimney is crumbling, and the paint is peeling. If you touch a window, a pane of glass is likely to fall out; duct tape is the repair tool of choice. When we arrive on the weekends, the mice look at us like "What the hell are you doing here?" and slowly saunter off under the furniture with exasperated expressions. Having had the entire place to themselves all week, they see no need to vacate for our sakes. I think "unbelievable rodent activity" is how the Orkin man described it. The house is in such disrepair it has a white-trash quality. We even boast the requisite broken-down vehicles. The only difference is that instead of old beat-up Chevys and Fords, we have broken-down Land Rovers and Porsches, complete with cinder-block pedestals.

Our yard is filled with more plastic fantastic than a Toys "Я" Us. We have every garage sale item Little Tikes ever made. You know the ones: the turtle sandbox, the log cabin playhouse, the slide, the orange and yellow car; they're all there, acting as a neon welcome sign to passing children. There are armies of bikes in every size and state of disrepair. All varieties of sporting equipment litter the lawn. As a testament to the overabundance of balls in my life, every possible type litters the yard. I do not recall which one of the boys became a bocce enthusiast, or what prompted us to install a tetherball pole, or the last time anyone played horseshoes, but should you want to engage in any of those games, or countless others, come on down. The entire scene looks like the French Quarter the day after Mardi Gras. Then there are the dangerous boy toys—the motorcycle, the go-cart, and—the ne plus ultra of all bone-breaking yard activities—the trampoline. These items tend to cause mothers with weaker constitutions to reverse out of the driveway as soon as they pull in, their children still safely strapped in their car seats. On some days,

I swear I can catch a glimpse of the personal-injury lawyers hiding in the bushes.

My boys have made friends with a family of home-schooled kids down the road. They live on an old working farm and they heat their farmhouse by burning logs in a woodstove and piling hay bales against the outer walls for insulation. Their water comes from a well on their property that often gets contaminated and becomes undrinkable when some random bit of wildlife gets in and drowns. Those kids are not allowed to play on our trampoline or ride the go-cart, because their mother thinks they are too dangerous. Meanwhile, on their property is a dilapidated barn with huge holes in the upper floor. If you were to fall through, you would drop straight down two stories to land on a row of hogs or a couple of dead pigeons and a pile of boards studded with rusty nails. If the barn doesn't do you in, you are sure to be zapped by one of the electrified wires hidden in the tall grass, or be butted by an angry goat. Despite being fed all the organic grains in the world, kids are still going to be goofy; her youngest once fastened a bungee cord to a tree branch in their yard, then proceeded to jump out of the tree with the other end in his mouth, managing to rip out half his teeth in the process. I guess we all have our own idea of what is dangerous.

The farm kids don't have television and though they do have a computer, it is for educational purposes only. They aren't allowed to play any of the popular online games, which their parents think are too violent. They are polite children, perhaps a bit socially awkward, but it's hilarious to overhear them playing a game of chase with my kids.

"When I catch you, I'm going to slit your throat and hang you up upside down by your feet until all your blood drains out! Then I'm going to skin you and butcher you and put you in the freezer until winter!"

You certainly don't learn that kind of talk from World of Warcraft.

AS YOU CAN IMAGINE, OUR PLACE IN THE COUNTRY IS A CHILD PAR-adise, to the likes of which apartment living cannot compare. City children love it here. So much, apparently, that on one Thursday afternoon I started receiving messages from various parents thanking me for inviting their kids up for the weekend. What? After the third mother (and fourth child) left a thank-you on our answering machine, I decided I had better investigate. I collared Peik and Truman, the only two old enough for unassisted sleepovers.

"Have you two been inviting friends for the weekend without asking me first?"

"Dude," Peik said, turning on Truman, "it's my week to have friends, not yours."

"According to whom?" I wanted to know.

"Mom," Truman shot back, "Peik always has friends. It's my turn."

"Well, I don't see how it's going to work. I will ask your father when he gets home." They both groaned, knowing this is what I usually say when I'm not going to give them what they want.

I have nothing against my boys having friends around. It's well worth any extra work, because when either Peik or Truman has company they are far less likely to spend the weekend trying to kill each other. Guests keep them out of my hair. They are particularly appealing in the country, where I can simply lock the door and let them in only for meals or the occasional emergency bathroom break, which does not include peeing. "Pee in the grass like you always do," I say through the screen of the locked door. Blake is usually around to make sure the boys don't burn down the outbuildings while creating some kind of AID (airborne incendiary device), and the motorcycle and go-cart usually break down before anyone has a chance to get hurt.

The problem with having four extra boys for the weekend is mainly a logistical one. As crazy as it may sound, on the weekend in question I decided I actually wanted all four kids to come along. If I could figure out how to transport and host them, perhaps some grateful mother would be willing to take a boy or three off my hands for an extended period, sort of a parenting karma payoff. But I am obliged to take along my already existing children; there is just no way to legally drive all this extra miniature manhood, too. Back in my day, we would just pile in the back of the station wagon, but Ralph Nader has ruined all that good clean fun, and the law requires me to provide each of these children with an actual seat and safety belt.

"Peter, we've got a problem." I turned to my husband to come up with a solution. It was Thursday night of a long week, so my synapses were not properly firing; there was no way I could solve this one. Peter's plan was simple. We made sure Blake was up for a crazy weekend, rented a second car, split up the crowd, and headed for the country.

I was awakened on Saturday morning by the sound of a go-cart and a dirt bike outside my bedroom window. Ah, the dulcet tones of boyhood. The very next thing I heard was someone yelling that the refrigerator had been unplugged sometime during the week and all the food had gone bad. Cleaning the fridge was the first of many disgusting tasks that

I would need to attend to over the weekend, but with Blake there I could face anything.

Our manny is the best of both worlds. He can be quite the outdoorsman, and is great for organizing things like campfires in the woods, or canoeing on the pond, but his gayness really comes in handy on the domestic side of things.

"We need to buy paper plates. Let's just feed everyone on paper plates all weekend," I said to him in an attempt to simplify things. Shopping, cooking, and cleaning up after three meals a day for nine boys and three adults was a daunting prospect.

"I looked at them, but I didn't buy any," he responded.

"I understand it will be hard for you," I said. "But I don't believe the boys have invited Martha Stewart, so we'll just have to use the ones from Christmas." Screw our carbon footprint. This was about survival.

We did, in fact, survive, though getting some of the boys to follow my plan of staying outside proved to be difficult. Some New York City kids have zero tolerance for the outdoors and are more comfortable experiencing it through a video screen. They love to watch baseball for four hours instead of strolling outside and picking up a bat and ball. If you can convince them to take a bike ride, they measure all distances in blocks.

"How many blocks to the covered bridge?"

"It's half a mile. There are no blocks in the country."

All in all, the kids were moderately well behaved—and no bones were broken, always a benchmark of success for me. The ultimate upside? For the next year, any time my boys ask to invite a friend I can say, "You just had friends up." Meanwhile, I am still awaiting that invitation from another mom to take my kids away.

———

MUCH LIKE A BELOVED DOG, MY TORTOISE, FRANK, TRAVELS WITH US to the country on the weekends, and when the weather is nice he spends his time outdoors in his own picket-fenced pen. He is very quiet, wandering in and out of rooms and traveling back and forth from the city to the country without complaint. He eats what he is given and is about as housebroken as anyone else in the family. He is essentially the perfect child. Is he cuddly? Not really, but after scraping kids off my body all day I welcome an animal that knows how to keep his distance.

One day in the country, Peter decided he wanted to take some movies of Frank with a new high-definition camera. He put Frank in the yard and filmed him walking around in excruciating detail. I'm not sure, but I think Peter was planning to have Frank be the next big star on Animal Planet. After taking a few minutes of footage, Peter left him outside his pen to go scout a different location. Tortoises are faster than you think, especially when you are not looking, and by the time Peter came back, Frank was nowhere to be found. I went ballistic.

"How could you lose Frank?" I yelled.

"He can't have gotten far," Peter weakly replied.

I pushed past him and out to the garage, where I grabbed a small chainsaw. I went to the area where Peter was now yelling Frank's name, as though a tortoise knows to come when called, and began mowing down bushes. I had no intention of stopping until either all eighteen acres were barren or we found Frank. You have to understand how attached I am to this tortoise. He is not one of those stinky water turtles that do nothing but generate lengthy discussions about whose turn it is to clean the algae-infested aquarium. Frank is a valued member of this family. We have had him for many years and watched him grow. He has height notches on the wall, like the other kids. This pet has a real personality, and he recognizes people. He greets me every morning in the kitchen, and he spends his afternoons next to me while I sew or write, soaking up the sunshine flooding in from the windows. A tortoise as perfect as Frank only comes around once in life, and the thought of losing him made me apoplectic.

After several hours of what can only be described as intense pruning, I gave up. Despondent, I went back into the house to have a cup of coffee and mourn my loss. I blamed Peter entirely; this was going to cost him our marriage—and he would have to take custody of the children. As I sat there fuming, Frank ambled out from behind one of Peter's oversize man speakers in the kitchen.

"Frank, you're here!" I was truly thrilled to see him. It seems that, like me, Frank is not a real outdoorsman. He's a city tortoise at heart, and had made his way back into the house.

"Hey, Chainsaw Charlie, you should have seen the look on your face." Peter laughed. "I've never seen you that concerned about any of the children."

"That's because Frank's never invited another tortoise up here without asking me first."

IT IS GREAT HAVING THE COUNTRY HOUSE TO GET AWAY TO ON weekends, but I wouldn't want to live there full-time. For one thing, there are no sidewalks, so my heels sink into the mud, which pretty much relegates me to the indoors with the tortoises and scared city children. For another, my connection to civilization—satellite TV—is tenuous. A couple of clouds and I am on my own. But mostly, I don't fit in with the locals. This is truly the land of antiquing and Birkenstocking, two activities not on my to-do list. There are plenty of New Yorkers who likewise make the trek to the Berkshires every weekend and infuse cash into the local economy, but we are generally regarded with disdain by the sandalistas, and I'm pretty sure we're subject to a separate price list for local services. It's a pity, this animosity, as there is quite a collection of interesting characters in the country, and I wouldn't mind getting to know them. For the most part, though, they prefer Peter; his eccentricity mysteriously makes them read him as one of them rather than one of us. Because of this, Peter learns things about the country that I will never find out first-hand.

Did you know that you need a permit to drive around with a dead body in your car? Or that it takes 120 pounds of dry ice to keep an unembalmed body from decomposing? Peter does. He was invited over when our neighbor Christopher performed a do-it-yourself funeral for his mother. After displaying the body in her bedroom on a bed of dry ice for several days, he drove her to the crematorium in the back of a borrowed station wagon. When his ninety-six-year-old father, Bill, died—Bill had played basketball with my kids right up until the end—Christopher took an even more active role: he helped with the actual cremation. I have heard of growing your own vegetables and even slaughtering your own Sunday roast, but cremating your own father? That's a bit too home-grown for me. Can you imagine sitting around a neighbor's house enjoying a cup of coffee and some conversation with a dead man packed in dry ice awaiting the pyre on the dining room table?

Apparently, Peter can. He may not have performed a DIY funeral on either of his parents, but he has come close.

Peter's mother, Peggy, loved her cat Heloise, or at least loved to make a fuss about her. (Apparently there was once an Abelard, but that was well before my time.) All day long, Peggy would scream from her bed: "Shut the door! The cat will get out!" or "Where's the cat? Have you let the cat escape?" She routinely whipped her homecare nurses into a panic. Keeping track of Heloise seemed to be her way of staying connected to the world as she was dying of cancer.

Peggy left Heloise to my daughter, Cleo. By that time, Heloise must have been quite old, but she was so petite and spry that we always thought of her as a kitten. We were all surprised when she began to slow down and eventually died.

Channeling the care Christopher gave his parents, Peter pulled out all the stops for the burial of Heloise. As her body lay covered, rotting in the grass, with an occasional dousing of bleach to ward off the maggots, Peter spent two days crafting her a slight mahogany coffin with meticulous dovetail joints and fancy brass hardware. When it was finally stained and polished to perfection, and Heloise was safely screwed inside, the funeral began. It was fit for a Kennedy. The children walked her coffin to our pet cemetery on a wagon covered with an American flag. There was a BB-gun salute—not twenty-one-gun, but at least twelve-gun—as her remains were lowered into the ground. When the soil was filled in, a lion statue was placed as a headstone. As I watched Peter's face, it occurred to me that taking such care to bury his mother's cat was actually his way of letting go of his mother.

—

I MAKE FUN OF DAIRY AIR AND PRETEND TO BE ON THE LOOKOUT for a better piece of property, but the truth is, this scruffy place works perfectly for our family. We sit on some of the most beautiful landscape in the Northeast, and Peter would have me living in a tent as long as the view was good. There is a mix of woods and fields and a lovely pond that freezes over in the winter, hard enough for us to convince ourselves it is safe for ice skating. Any other time of year, the pond reflects the colors of the spectacular sunsets that melt into the Taconic Mountains. In the fall, the country is downright Rockwel-lesque, with the color of the changing leaves displayed in about a thousand different hues. The place looks especially picturesque in the winter, when a pristine blanket of snow turns the crap on the lawn into a wonderland of sculpture and our leaky heating produces a perfect row of icicles along the eaves. We could never leave, anyway, with Heloise planted firmly in the pet cemetery. So here I stay, and perhaps one day I will uncover for myself all the hidden potential.

"How did girls get lapped when they had such a
clear lead?"

BOYS WILL BE BOYS

I MUST HAVE BEEN JACK THE RIPPER, OR PERHAPS Lucrezia Borgia, in a previous life, since in this one I have been sentenced to life in a two-bedroom apartment with six males. Cleo escaped early on in search of female companionship—her choice of an all-girl boarding school not in the least accidental. Devoid of her feminine charms, my close quarters are populated with a gender I am incapable of understanding. I wouldn't describe myself as a girly-girl, but I do enjoy all the accoutrements that come with being me: the jewelry, the makeup, and of course the shoes. If I lived in a house full of five little girls I would be in heaven. I would sew little matching dresses for all of us and our dolls, purchase exquisite tiaras from the shop down the street, and teach them how to use sex as a weapon and Google-stalk ex-boyfriends. We'd have tea parties, of course, and once we perfected our manners we would take field trips to places like the Plaza or Serendipity, or hell, even American Girl, just to show off our raised pinky fingers. Had I known that my girl time was going to be so fleeting, I would have let Cleo wear that damn pink princess tutu to school every day if that was what her little heart desired.

Instead, I am awash in a sea of camouflage. I step lightly through my apartment in four-inch heels, as careful as a bomb defuser in a minefield, trying to avoid the neck-breaking toys scattered everywhere. Some items I recognize—bikes, skateboards, Rollerblades: typical childhood fare. Others scare the bejesus out of me, like the thing that has three wheels and requires swaying hips to propel it, and the sneakers with the hidden wheels that seem to pop up only at busy intersections and always at the moment when the light turns yellow midway through the crossing. I'm quite fond of the full-size scooters that fold up into sleek bundles worthy of Inspector Gadget, but these objects are more usually found perilously leaning against a wall, ready to slip into my path and carve a gash in my ankle at the slightest provocation. I had just gotten used to my constant terror of skateboards when Peik rolled into the apartment with his broken in half.

"Oh, my God, it's finally happened," I said, putting a hand over my eyes. "You've killed someone with that thing, haven't you?"

"Chillax, Mom," he replied, stepping up onto the board, swiveling his ankles gracefully, and moving the contraption over to the couch, stopping only when he had slammed it into the coffee table. "It's my new wave board."

"As if your old skateboard wasn't dangerous enough, you have to bring this thing into my house?" I yelled, but he'd already reinserted his earphones and was off showing the other boys how to kill themselves at twenty miles per hour in an entirely novel and irresistible way. I didn't need to watch; I knew they were all drooling like a pack of knuckle-dragging Neanderthals being shown the wheel for the first time.

As I picked my way back across the Mekong Delta to stock up on bandages for the inevitable "Mom! I'm bleeding!" about to be announced, I had to remind myself of the other danger, the one overhead. About three years ago I made a recording of my voice that says "Don't play baseball in the house," and Peter put it on a loop that now plays constantly. Even so, if my boys can find a way to nail me in the head with a small stitched leather projectile "by accident," they will strive to do it. I dodge enough of these, and the next thing you know a basketball lands on my keyboard. After years of hostile negotiations with the downstairs neighbors, we have decreed that a basketball may not touch the floor—I have expelled many of these orange orbs from my house, yet, like cockroaches, they keep getting back in. Luckily this one was a blow-up version, so I took my letter opener and dispatched it to its next life. On my way into the kitchen to dispose of the corpse, I was nailed in the butt by a plastic hockey puck, which should have been the last straw; but, believe it or not, I have reached a level of Zen that will slowly evolve into Alzheimer's, and then it is I who will crash my electric wheelchair into their furniture and maniacally throw balls at my grown children as they try to wipe dinner off *my* chin.

—

IN THEIR WAKING HOURS, THE PACK NEVER STOPS MOVING. WHEN they are not attached to wheels or balls, they tumble through the apartment as a giant mass of wrestling bodies, usually with the large ones on the bottom and the small ones on top, continuing in this manner until one of them needs to file a grievance with the Don't Bleed on My New Couch Department of I Don't Care. If the injury sustained is serious enough, then we hunt down the child-appropriate Lenox Hill Hospital Frequent Flyer Card and head off to the emergency room. Split chins I will try to mend with crazy glue and butterfly bandages, but if that doesn't staunch the bleeding I turn the damage over to the professionals. The triage doctors not only know us by names and birthdates but have also memorized our ten-digit insurance group number, just to make sure we have a speedy visit. And when the treated child returns home you would think he had won both the Purple Heart and the Silver Star. The brothers gather together and a hearty round of "I got more stitches than you did" and "Remember when you gave me this scar" begins. It's like watching a Disney version of *The Deer Hunter.*

Last week, Pierson came home missing one of his front teeth. It had finally fallen out at school, after weeks of him pulling on it and twisting on it and pushing on it and letting it dangle by a fleshy thread, but remaining completely incapable of just yanking the damn thing out. Someone had carefully placed the relic in a plastic tooth-shaped container and laced it onto a string around Pierson's neck. In public school you're lucky if they let you go to the bathroom, rinse the blood off the tooth, and carefully fold it into a brown paper towel. In private school they make jewelry out of the moment.

"Hey, look," Pierson said with a grin, walking over to Peik to show off this proud, if dubious, accomplishment.

"Nice necklace," he replied before cocking back his arm and knocking out the remaining front tooth. To be fair, Peik was really doing all of us a favor, as the tooth was already superloose and nobody wanted to go through the hell of another week hearing about Pierson's teeth. It was so far gone the gum didn't even bleed; Pierson just stood there, looking at the object in his hand until a lightbulb went on over his head.

"Thankths," he lisped to his brother before turning to me, pink with excitement. "Thith ith big, Mom! I lotht two in one day! Do you think the Tooth Fairy will give me a bonuth? I bet she hath never theen the liketh of thith before." By bedtime the teeth were nowhere to be found, but the Tooth Fairy took pity and left a bonus anyway. I don't mind her paying a premium for lost teeth, because the money she leaves ends up in the laundry room the next day and I just fold it right back into my purse, in wait for the next big tooth event.

THE ONLY THINGS BOYS SEEM TO LOVE MORE THAN WHEELS, BALLS, and stitches are their own penises. Back in my day it was shocking when Michael Jackson and Madonna grabbed their groin in a music video, but these days my boys call that dancing. Every time they hear music, they clutch their crotches and hang on for dear life—it's shockingly Pavlovian. I don't have a penis, I don't even like to say the word "penis," and I will never understand the fascination my sons have with theirs or why they need to hold on to them like handles. Constantly. Everywhere I look around there is a boy who needs to put his pants on and his penis away. Like the little hominids in the American Museum of Natural History, they walk around completely exposed with no sense of shame. Even in their sleep, they're captivated by their weenies: when I enter the room to wake them up in the morning, I am greeted with multiple woodies, all pointing at me as if I were a heroine in a demented Hitchcock film. I know it's normal and natural and all that, but why me?

Talking about sex with my boys is unfathomable, but when Peik came home from health class with a rubber and a banana as homework, I figured I'd better find my depth. The week before, he had brought home his crowd of boys and girls after school and gone into the boys' bedroom, locking the door behind them.

About an hour later, Peter prodded me. "Go in there and check on them," he said.

"No way. You go."

"It's your turn."

"Cleo was my turn," I said. "It will be my turn again when Finn is thirteen." I went back to my sewing, and Peter went back to his stock market analysis. We were at a parenting stalemate: each pretending that they didn't desperately want the other to be the one their child hates for having interrupted the teen orgy. A minute ticked by, then another.

"Fine," I said, losing this particular game of chicken. "What could they be doing, anyway? There are ten of them in there." Under my safety-in-numbers nonchalance was a vivid image of the mythical rainbow party, as featured on *Oprah*. I meekly gave two knocks on the door, and an even longer two minutes later Peik opened it a crack, peering out with one wild eye.

"What?" he snapped. I deserved that.

"You need any snacks in there?" I held out the half-eaten

bag of Goldfish crackers I'd grabbed on my way as an excuse, as though knocking in the first place weren't humiliating enough. As far as I could tell, all the clothes were on and normal fourteen-year-old activities were under way: Web surfing, guitar strumming, truth-or-daring. Peik just glared at me. "Sorry?" I whispered and he gave me a half smile of sympathy before snugging the door closed in my face.

This incident clarified my need to have an open dialogue with my eldest son. Determined to overcome my fear, I turned to the Internet. Cleo had been so much easier; she learned everything on the street, like a normal child, and brought the information home to me without embarrassment. Besides, she has parts I understand and sympathize with. Period? No problem. Wet dream? Gross. The advice I found in the ether was disheartening. Start early, one site suggested: "When teaching your toddler where his nose and toes are, include 'This is your penis' in your routine." Great; now I needed to teach the toddler something he clearly already knew as a birthright? Thanks, Mr. Internet. "Use the correct terms to avoid confusion. Say things like 'Girls have a vulva and a vagina, and boys have a penis and testicles.'" What's so confusing about "weenie"? Do balls really need to be called testicles? I tried this approach and started only using the word "penis"—so as not to be *confusing*—but my attempts went awry by way of my kindergartener's principal's office.

"Why did you say 'penis' in the middle of circle time?" Mrs. Mackenzie asked Larson.

"I just had to" was his reply. Her solution? He was required to come to her office five minutes early every day and say "penis" as many times as he needed to get it out of his system. Then he could return to class and join in good clean fun. After three days, his Tourettian outbursts stopped and he resumed his routine. Perhaps I can find a website that tells me to say things like "This is how you masturbate," and the boys can then go on a cleansing routine of getting that out of their systems once and for all, as well. But hey, who are we kidding? In a world where "penis" is still considered a curse word in kindergarten, are we really getting anywhere when it comes to talking openly about sex with our children?

I could have quit, but I take my motherly responsibilities seriously, so I pushed on. Another site blithely suggested, "If you feel uncomfortable talking to your children about sex, recruit an uncle or a male friend to discuss the subject with your child," as though Amber alerts were merely a ruse to slow down traffic on the thruway. All this advice did for me was conjure up images of Chester the Molester and Jeffrey Dahmer. Okay, I'll be sure to try *that one*. Maybe I could ask a "male friend" along the lines of my husband, I thought. He's got a penis. I looked over at him, asleep on the couch in front of a Formula One race, remote in one hand, the other lightly resting on his crotch. How did these people ever come to be in charge of the world? This is something I often ask myself. How did men surpass women in status, power, and wealth? These questions come from a place of love, mind you. I live with far too many of them to survive day-to-day existence while harboring any ill feeling. But I will admit that I don't understand men, and that I consistently find women to be the more capable sex. As early as the age of two, girls leave boys standing bewildered in their dust as they speed along the social, emotional, and intellectual racecourse of life.

Cleo did everything earlier and better than any of the boys; as a group, they were slow to walk and talk, refused to give up breastfeeding at a reasonable age, and were impossible to potty train. They still can't take a poop without yelling for help, and they can't even manage to get all their urine consistently in the toilet. Can anyone explain why it is so hard to pee into something the size of a platter with something the size of a cocktail sausage? If I had known good aim violated the laws of physics, I would have trained them to sit down while they pee. They can sit when they poop, so clearly it's not out of the question. I have noticed that most of them stand in front of the toilet, hands on their hips, penis thrust in the direction of the toilet as they release their man water. "Oh really?" I yell at them. "You choose this moment to not touch the damn thing!?" How is this evolved? How is this the dominant gender?

Since Cleo was four she has fixed herself meals, uncomplicated things like breakfast and small snacks. I can't begin to imagine one of my boys—much less Peter—taking such proactive measures to conquer hunger.

"Mom, can I have some cereal?" Peik asks me every single morning.

"Sure," I say.

Like clockwork, fifteen minutes later he starts whining. "Mom, I'm hungry. Aren't you going to get my cereal?"

"Is your arm broken?"

"Don't you love me enough to feed me?"

"Didn't I feed you yesterday?" I rejoin, petting him like a prize Pekingese. "Isn't that proof enough of my undying love for you, my oldest son, the fruit of my loins, the jewel in my crown?"

"Okay, okay." He sulks off, rolling his eyes. "I'll get it myself."

They can't overcome hunger, and yet they are given the red phone, the suitcase with the codes, the absolute power of world nuclear annihilation. That seems practical.

Sometimes I think Truman may be my one bright spot—my chance at being shown that men aren't all nincompoops. But as bright as he is, he can never, ever, *ever* do his homework without a cattle prod pushing at him.

"Mom, I have to do my homework," he says, hours after the initial broadcast about how he needs to do his homework.

"Okay," I say again, "So do it."

"I need you to help me." He slumps in front of the unopened book, the blank notebook. I walk over and uncrumple the moist homework assignment sheet clutched in his hand, put the pencil in his other hand, and open the textbook to the page designated. I then walk away.

"There. Now I have helped you. Let me know when you're actually doing it and get stuck. Until then, you're on your own."

I never even knew that Cleo had homework until it came back to the apartment in her backpack, all dolled up with stars and stickers. She never once asked me to acquire special materials for her school projects; she was completely self-sufficient.

After about an hour of sitting in front of his homework, playing air drums with his pencils, Truman Moms me again.

"Mom, I think it says here that I need to build a diorama of a Native American village for social studies class. I think it says that it's due tomorrow." He doesn't meet my eyes, and his start to faintly glisten.

"How long have you known?" I ask him.

"That's not fair," he says. "What difference does that make? It's still due tomorrow." He is about to burst at this point. Of course, I have known for a week, because another kid in his class has a mother who practically does the projects for her child—or, more precisely, enlisted the help of other moms with an email blast that started with "Do any of you sew?" I can't let my boys off that easy; what if I'm not around the day they need to put together their own assault rifle in a godforsaken trench somewhere because some male heads of state couldn't work things out?

I let Truman suffer in silence one long moment more before pulling out my magic bag of pipe cleaners and felt. "Go get the glue gun," I say, and his face instantly brightens. I figure he did stay up with me all those nights watching *Project Runway* and encouraged me to go audition, so staying up into the wee hours to build a replica of Manhattan is the least I can do in return.

The multitask gene clearly rests on the X chromosome, as I know of no men who can do more than one thing at a time. Peter routinely gets up from the sofa and wanders into the kitchen for a snack, not even thinking that it might be a good idea to carry with him on his voyage the detritus from the snack he made fifteen minutes earlier. He can amass up to ten coffee cups around his home workspace before Zoila corrals them into the dishwasher. He is a highly intelligent, award-winning architect, but he can never leave the house on time in the morning because he can never find his keys. I can't even count the times per week he has to put out an all-points bulletin on his eyeglasses. It would make sense to develop a system by which he could remember where these essential items are. A hook by the door? A string on his glasses? A chain that connects his wallet to his belt loop? And his kind run the world?

How many times while I've expressed my concern over some alarmingly backward behavior in one of my guys has a sympathetic mother said, "Well, you do know that Einstein didn't speak until he was four?" And how many of these mothers have only girls? Five minutes of observing Larson's preschool class is all the proof I need that little girls are superior. They complete sentences and play elaborate games of imagination, assigning roles to one another with alacrity. With an innate understanding of exactly what they want, the girls take charge of the room, organizing cubbies and dressing themselves in color-coordinated outfits, complete with shoes they have actually tied themselves. Peik still needs Velcro. Who tied boys' shoes before that clever invention? Off in a corner, a clutch of boys is calling each other monosyllabic names as they play with a blue train with a face. Have you noticed that girls have the good sense to avoid toys that endlessly go in circles to nowhere? Trust me, I know I'm not dealing with Einstein in any of my boys; I don't need to be comforted by the not-so-novel idea that a slow starter can end up on the path of genius. Besides, I bet that Einstein had his mother tie his shoes on the way out the door to college and that she was still wiping up the linoleum around the toilet every time he paid her a visit as a grown man.

I'm not the only one puzzled by how boys become men and then men become the masters of the universe. I have yet to meet a single mother on a park bench, a female teacher, or a pediatrician who doesn't have the same thoughts. It's only the men who disagree with me and feel the need to support their counterthesis by listing every accomplishment of every male in history. The only possible explanation I can come up with is that in prehistoric times women needed some space to get the real work done without having to worry about the crotch-grabbing spectacle over on the pile of furs. So the women gave men bows and arrows and taught them how to hunt, and eventually when they got tired of shooting their little weapons at animals they shot at other men, and war began, and then men had something to do with their time. The trend stuck. Whatever the case, I love my boys. I find their antics and inabilities amusing and constantly surprising. I just don't get how they ever lapped girls when the fairer sex had such a clear lead.

"I'm not the outdoorsy type, unless a waiter is
following me with a tray of champagne."

WANDERLUST

"HOW DO YOU FEEL ABOUT KENYA?" PETER asked me on the phone, asking me out on our second official date.

"I love Kenya!" I said. Of course, I thought he was joking—who gets immunizations to go on a date? But no, he was completely serious. This is why I love New York; where else can you meet a man with the means and the sense of adventure to plan such a killer date?

Peter called the New York offices of Ker & Downey, an old-school safari company, and told them we wanted to take a week-long safari and would like to leave the coming weekend.

"But it's Tuesday. You want to leave Saturday?" the agent asked in disbelief.

"Or Friday," Peter replied casually.

"People plan a trip like this a full year in advance. Kenya is in Africa. There are a lot of arrangements to make."

Peter messengered a check over to prove he was serious, reservations were made, and I found myself in the office of a tropical infectious disease specialist getting vaccinations and malaria pills. The next stop was a whirlwind shopping spree for fabulous khaki cocktail wear. Peter already wears khaki, so his wardrobe was perfect. I mailed my daughter to Texas to stay with my mom, and we headed for the airport.

It was a dream date from start to finish. We stayed at the Governors' Camp in the Masai Mara, where we could hear lions roar as we lay in our luxury tent. One afternoon I was changing and heard someone enter. I turned around to see a wild elephant standing about ten feet from me. I grabbed my camera and got a priceless close-up of his face. Only after the camera flashed did I notice the panicked guard with the spear who shooed the powerful creature out.

"You will live a long life because you were not killed by that elephant," the guard informed me. It hadn't occurred to me that I wasn't on an amusement park ride.

We then went to a camp called Borana, where the animators of *The Lion King* stayed for inspiration. One day our guide called us over to the edge of a precipice.

"Come see this." He motioned. On a small cliff below were two sleeping leopards.

"This is very rare. Leopards are difficult to see because they hunt only at night and are well camouflaged. They are solitary animals; seeing two together is very rare. It only happens when they are mating." When we turned around, there was a waiter holding a tray of champagne. Thank God my backpacking days through Europe with a Eurail Pass eurocard are over, I thought; *this* is travel.

That night, back at the camp, we dined with an Italian expat wearing a shoulder-holstered pistol who showed us his elephant gun with lion tooth marks in the butt. It occurred to me that he wasn't on a photo safari like the rest of us.

"Let's all have a drink to congratulate Peter and Laura," our host said. "They are the first guests here at Borana ever to see all of the big five in one trip. We have guests who return year after year in the hopes of such an accomplishment." The "big five" are the elephant, lion, water buffalo, rhino, and leopard. Unbeknownst to us, it is the goal of a safari to view these animals, or bag them if that's your thing.

"Why not the giraffe, or the hippo?" I asked our host.

"The animals in the big five were determined by big-game hunters. These are the animals most difficult to shoot, because of their ferocity when cornered," he said.

I still enjoyed seeing the giraffe the most, but it was our friends the mating leopards that gave us the edge. I love it when I win competitions I didn't even know I was entered in.

After Borana, we stayed at Giraffe Manor in Nairobi, a 140-acre estate used as a refuge for giraffes. The giraffes roam free on the property and, like park squirrels, they stick their heads in through the dining room windows to beg for food.

Peter must have known this trip would be a hard act to follow, especially after we took our cue from the leopards. He had me at "safari," and I never looked back. Oh, sure, we went to Europe a couple of times to visit my brother's family, and I have been known to tag along on the occasional business trip, but once we had two three four five six kids, "vacation" became a four-letter word.

Once. We have gone on vacation all together, as a family of eight exactly once. I'm not really sure why we did it— perhaps because Peter had traveled a good deal as a child and wanted his children to do the same, or maybe because I was suffering from some form of wanderlust postpartum depression. We decided on Puerto Rico as it was a short, direct flight, and we could give the kids a taste of *olde* architecture without me needing to schlep them around for passport pictures while still sorting out Baby White Male's paperwork. In a fit of "what to pack," I went onto the L. L. Bean website and ordered a bunch of polo shirts and shorts in assorted sizes, some swim trunks, and flip-flops. When they arrived I opened the box and dumped the contents into a wheelie. Six hours later, the eight of us were in Old San Juan.

Remember when the Brady Bunch go to Hawaii and Bobby and Peter find some ugly idol at Dad Brady's construction site and it turns out the trinket has an "evil taboo" and the next thing you know Bobby's head almost gets bashed in by a hotel wall decoration, then Greg has a massive wipeout on his surfboard and Peter is attacked by a vicious tarantula while he is sleeping? And then they have to return the cursed thing to the "Tiki Cave," where crazy Vincent Price is lurking and tries to scare them, then ties them up, while back at the hotel the girls confess to knowing where the boys are and oh why didn't they tell their parents sooner? And finally it's all happily ever after with a big luau and everybody—Vince included—takes a turn "sounding the horn of brotherhood" while blowing into a big conch shell and great hilarity ensues? Well, Puerto Rico was nothing like any of that. It rained. We stood in line for a boat to the recreation island. I suspect the food was shipped in from Wendy's. The kids swam in the pool during the one hour it didn't rain. We could have gone to the

Holidome in Paramus and been a thousand times happier and about $15,000 up on tuition.

Peter worries that we don't travel enough. But having children in such a wide range of ages makes vacation planning tricky. It's hard to find a destination that appeals to all of them. My older children should be receiving their requisite doses of culture by touring the great cities of Europe. I am loath to imagine the horror of shepherding my three younger ones through the British Museum or the Louvre. We have all grown to love the *Winged Victory of Samothrace* without a head, but I can't promise that after my crew blew through she wouldn't be missing a wing. Maybe we should wait until the boys will eat something other than chicken nuggets. Or till I can be sure I won't be arrested for creating an international incident when one of them hocks a loogie off the Eiffel Tower, killing a Frenchman in the process.

Last summer Peter's friend John took his family to a dude ranch in Wyoming. Knowing I am not the outdoor type, unless a waiter is following me with a tray of champagne, Peter decided to take Peik and Truman for a session of male bonding. Or male bondage, depending on your deftness with the reins. I'm not sure why he agreed to go to a ranch; his only memory from the single such childhood trip was of his father's butt bleeding from too much riding. Nevertheless, he picked up the phone and booked a week in August.

My inner calendar shrieked—August is the darkest month in New York, when both nannies and therapists leave the city. It is a dangerous time, with hollow-eyed mommies pushing strollers and sobbing into cell phones, begging their therapist's receptionist to please, *please,* have him return the call. If I was not mistaken, I had just been sentenced to five days alone with a two-, a five-, and a six-year-old. Outnumbered by the wee digits. Sure, I could take them up to Dairy Air, but then I'd be even *more* alone with them. At least in the city I don't have to worry about one of them drowning in the pool while I'm pulling another out of a mangled dune buggy. Not one to be outdone by a spouse, I turned to the mouse and made a snap decision of my own: we would go on a Disney cruise! Who doesn't love Disney? Cleo would join us and I would plop the boys into day care mousetivities and have some real mother-daughter bonding time, placidly reading our books next to the grown-ups-only pool.

Here's one thing you should know about the Disney Cruise: the culture of Disney is insidious. Mousack is piped into every nook and cranny of the damn ship: the elevators, the restaurants, the hallways. If you submerge yourself in the mouse-shaped pool, you will hear the haunting theme from *The Little Mermaid,* as though she were down there, some-where, *singing.* You can't escape it by going to the Lido deck, or even, God forbid, your own room. Every single time you leave your cabin, some sort of switch is triggered so that upon reentry the radio is back on, blaring "Small World." I thought the Geneva Convention had banned that song. If they want to find Bin Laden so badly, the government should just turn Afghanistan over to Disney and the company can pipe some of its greatest hits into the terrorists' caves. Before you know it, every last one of them will crawl out and confess to some-thing, *anything,* to make it stop.

But I'm getting ahead of myself. Before we could even set foot on the good ship Disney, I had to find a way to get the three Mouseketeers to the launching pad down in Florida. I had assumed this would be one flight, but no, it was two, and the last thing you want to do when traveling with the smallest of children is have to switch planes in Atlanta. I was tempted to fly Cleo up from Texas just to help me ease the pain, but I decided I could do this, and I could even *love* doing it.

Things began to unravel at La Guardia Airport, where I was informed that you could no longer check bags at the curb because the airlines had decided to charge a new fee for any checked baggage. Which meant we had to get into a long snaking line in order to turn over our unwieldy luggage. Have you done this with a toddler? Well, have you done it with a toddler, a special-needs kid, and a pushy six-year-old? Pierson tried to help by manning the stroller, meaning he decided to ram it into the backs of my legs every time the fellow in front of us moved so much as an inch. I prefer to let a little space open up before I have to shoulder all the bags and precariously tip the oversize wheelie forward. Pierson, on the other hand, is incrementally driven.

"Mom, move up," he'd say. *Ram.*

"Chill out." I'd try not to curse at him. "I'm trying to figure out where Larson is."

"He's up there, pretending to be with those people."

And he was. Clearly embarrassed by our steerage situation, Larson had found a young couple in the first-class express line who looked vaguely like him. He was loitering just out of their peripheral vision, lightly stroking their YSL luggage. I think he might have ended up in a much grander locale, if I'd let him.

We made it through security okay, even with the task of having to remove all our shoes and get them back on again, and waiting at the gate to board was fine, especially as it was the first time the boys had access to my carefully packed activity bag. They were enthralled by the new dot-to-dots and fresh crayons. Even Finn seemed as though he might be ready for his mid-morning nap by the time we got on the plane. No such luck. The minute we boarded, all hell broke loose. Along with "Never admit fatigue," "Fight over the window seat" is one of the two cardinal rules of childhood, and Pierson and Larson immediately obeyed it. Sleepy little pre-boarding Finn turned into a cute version of that animated creature Gollum from *Lord of the Rings:* standing on armrests, dancing on tray tables, and just generally trying to scramble over other people and suitcases and into the aisle, a demented gleam in his eye. I opened a bag of Cheetos, hoping it would work its usual magic. He grabbed it and flung them everywhere at once. Larson and Pierson stopped squabbling long enough to laugh at me picking orange bits out of my hair and then went after the rest of the contents of the activity bag, spilling the Model Magic wrappers and fuzzy colored pipe cleaners from a "Make Your Own Bug" Kit. The big, brightly painted wooden beads provided for the bodies went rolling off to a faraway row. Gollum stood up on my lap and played peek-a-boo with the elderly couple behind us. I felt sorry for them. A smiling two-year-old is adorable for exactly three "I see yous"; after that, you tend to want your space back. I would have gotten him his own seat, but how could I when I needed to have a hand on the other two?

Across the aisle a couple in their late thirties sat down, clutching the same Disney Cruise Line travel packet as I had. It was just the two of them, no children. I had to ask.

"Why? Why are you going on a Disney Cruise without children? Young at heart? What the hell?"

"Not by choice," the man answered, good-naturedly. "My sister is getting remarried and wants her children to have fun at the wedding."

"Oh, thank God," I said, pitying them but comforted to hear a valid excuse. Just then the "Fasten Seat Belts" sign hinged on and we started to taxi, eliciting from Pierson the now-predictable wail *"I have to pee!"* I had asked him seven billion times, but no, this was when he decided he would definitely die if his bladder wasn't emptied immediately. I tried to soothe him for the excruciating five minutes it took to reach get-up-and-walk-around altitude, but by then he had decided he didn't have to pee after all and would instead wait until the drink carts were blocking the aisles in either direction and the passengers in the row in front of us had unanimously decided that ten A.M. was the best time to snooze, and so had reclined right into my personal space.

"I really have to pee!" Pierson shouted from the window seat, grasping his crotch and doing a little dance in the three inches of space allotted him. I assessed the drink cart traffic jam.

"You're going to have to wait," I said, shushing him. Finn had finally exhausted himself and was asleep across my lap. Any sudden movements by others or me would surely result in another round of Hobbit-chasing.

"Let me just pee in a cup, then," he whispered, which sent Larson into fits of laughter. Mercifully, the drink cart cleared at that moment. Pierson walked from armrest to armrest over us all and into the aisle, racing to the back of the plane and disappearing into the john. Larson gave me an impish look and scooted over to the window, pushing his brother's crap into the middle seat.

THANK GOD CLEO WAS THERE IN ORLANDO TO HELP US GET ONTO the shuttle, because by then I was ready to turn around and fly home, solo. The guides packed us onto the Disney-fied bus and immersed us in the culture: a soaking that wouldn't stop for the next three days. I sensed danger and gave my boys one last bit of advice: if anyone offers you something called Kool-Aid, don't drink it. Disney is a worthy opponent, with many ways of indoctrinating malleable minds into the cult. They use such techniques as tanned crew members in crispy uniforms, with overwrought, laminated smiles and enthusiastic voices, two-finger pointing you along the way to fun.

On board, it was all Disney, all the time. Cleo was strangely but cautiously enchanted at first, sucked in by the cleverly executed sculptures of the Little Mermaid, Belle, Cinderella, and the other Disney princesses scattered around the hallways. Getting to our room was no small feat: every couple of steps some creature in a towering costume would pop out of the woodwork, frightening my young boys. Finn was clinging to me like a monkey, face tucked firmly into my dress. Larson stayed behind me, while Pierson would occasionally check in with me, dubious.

"Mom, did you see that duck?" he'd ask.

"You mean Donald?" I'd say.

"He has a name? Donald? That's stupid."

"Well, he was named back around the Depression, when Donald wasn't such a stupid name as it is today. You know what's worse? His middle name is *Fauntleroy.*"

"What about that tall guy with the long ears? What's his name?"

"Goofy."

"Seriously, Mom. Goofy? Is that supposed to be funny?"

"You know, Mom," Cleo interjected, "you could let them watch age-appropriate cartoons now and then."

"Trust me," I said, "If we were on the *Family Guy* cruise, they'd know everyone here."

"Is Petah heah?" Larson yelled from his shelter, having

caught only the salient points of the conversation and jumping up and down with the most joy he had shown thus far. "Wheah, wheah? And Stewie?"

"See," I said, opening the door to our cabin. It was clean, tidy, and creepy. Done up in faux-deco black and white, it used the Mousetif everywhere: curtains with brass Mickey tie-back pegs, Minnie-shaped soaps in the loo, a kid's table in the familiar trisphered shape; even tiny little mouse heads worked into the very woof and weave of the carpet under our feet! The place was infested with mice. Shimmery little satiny mouse heads were brocaded onto the duvets—and, most insidious of all, a collection of framed "family" photos adorned the tiny desk. At first glance I thought maybe the cruise people had pulled images of us off the Web—that would have been freaky enough. But no, these were pictures of Walt and family: on his wedding day, at the opening of Disneyland in California, on the deck of a similar-looking ship. It brought to mind the closing shot of *The Shining,* when the camera focuses in on the black-and-white photo of Jack Nicholson, who has joined the many dead of the old resort hotel, and you see that he's grinning because he's so happy to have been sucked into their world. At least I could comfort myself with the thought that the mom and kid got out of that hellhole alive.

For a moment I flashed on an image of Peter, Peik, and Truman, saddling up horses and riding out into the wilderness, with no mice for miles. Or at least, no mice wearing shoes. I could almost smell the pot of beans simmering over the open campfire. Ah, simplicity. Oh, food.

Food is absolutely everywhere. You can't take a mouse-kastep without running into a restaurant of some kind. Care to visit Goofy's Galley? Maybe Pluto's Dog House? (Who would

eat the food in a doghouse, I ask you?) Or perhaps Pinocchio's
Pizzeria? The pool deck is surrounded by mini themed food
stands. My kids, who are normally not big eaters, were instantly
overwhelmed by the lure of "free food."

"You mean we can have anything on the menu, for free?"
Pierson grinned. He was mesmerized by the variety and the
ease with which everything appeared. You just walked up to
the counter and asked. No negotiations, no exchange of
money. The pancakes, naturally, were mouse-shaped. The
French toast was seared with the brand of Mickey. Even the
ketchup was rendered onto the plate in three round squirts:
one big, two smaller on top. Mouse.

On day two, the novelty had not yet worn off. I watched
Larson pull himself out of the ear part of the pool, skitter over
to a fake grass hut, order a burger with fries, and deliver it to
our poolside table, giggling deliriously. He had no intention of
eating it; he'd gotten it just because he could. No parental in-
volvement necessary. Ten minutes later, he went back and ordered a hot dog, to make sure he wasn't dreaming. Nearby, the
lure of self-serve soft-serve ice cream nearly undid Pierson,
who by the end of the afternoon had stood in line countless
times to concoct yet another version of Freudian Fantasia. Not
to be outdone by himself, he also managed to mix about fifteen different "all new" soda flavors from the easy-access noz-
zles. How about a Pink Lemonade–Fruit Punch–Cola with a
dash of Sprite this time? He brought each to me the way a cat
brings a dead mouse to the door—with pride and insistence
that I acknowledge how precious my son's ability to jerk soda
had become. So much for "Drop your kids off and have some
quiet time by the pool." I was only ever able to drop Finn anywhere, as Larson and Pierson required my attentive response
to each and every new discovery. At least I got some quality

time with Cleo, bonding with her over the absurdity of her little brothers.

"Why do they do that?" I asked her, after one of the boys almost fell into the pool while trying to avoid some costumed character. Other kids went up to Cinderella or Snow White as if approaching celebrities, holding out little books to collect all the various autographs.

"Two reasons," Cleo observed. "One, they are boys. They have never seen any of the girl movies, and Disney these days is mostly for girls, except for Nemo, and it would freak a kid out to see a full-size Nemo, out of water. Second, you have nothing but disdain for sugar-coated fantasy. You have created them in your own image."

"That is not true," I said, but Cleo was right. I like my fantasy dark and brooding, draped in cobwebs and with skeletons popping up out of it. So do my boys. Without trying to, I had trained them to mistrust good and to embrace the darker side of things. Was that so bad? "I'll prove it to you, I'm going to take them on this 'Private Island' tour—see?" I pointed to a very Jim Jones–ish stop on the cruise, where you are actually let off the ship and encouraged to explore palm trees and a fiberglass pirate vessel anchored offshore. "They will love this."

Cleo rolled her eyes.

"I will love this," I retorted.

I hated it. But I tried not to show it. I strapped on my lowest-heel espadrilles and gamely herded the boys off the boat and onto the shore, overriding their lazy complaints about how they just wanted to stay by the pool and make more ice cream and sodas—maybe even ice cream floats! What might chocolate and Sprite taste like together? They had to know! Luckily, there was more free food on the beach, and even an

actual bar with actual booze so I could wrap a warm fuzzy
blanket of alcohol around my mouse-numbed brain.

The last day I did try to get all the kids to go to mousetivities, but by the afternoon we were all back by the pool, once
again being regaled with looping Disney cartoons on the
JumboTron (or was that DumboTron? It honestly might have
been) overhead. Children with lesser fortitude might have
caved, but after three days mine had had enough magic and
dreams come true. "Mom, I want to go home," Pierson said,
drawing a tear of pride from my eye.

Once off the ship at eight A.M., we were all raring to get
those two plane trips out of the way and be back home in
time for an early dinner and a couple of episodes of *The Simpsons.* Our flight from Orlando arrived in Atlanta just in time
to connect to the 2:40 flight to La Guardia. Make that 3:45.
Oh, we meant 4:40. Well, maybe 6:15. Actually, it was looking more like 7:30. Cleo was already back in Houston, and I
was again kicking myself that I hadn't made her suffer this
part of the trip by my side. The delays were accompanied by
a game of musical gates, some which required a tram ride to
another terminal, all of which required me to break camp and
move the three caballeros along. A toddler, much like a
puppy, can only be expected to stay cooped up for a limited
amount of time. I had to let Finn out of his restraints every
now and then, which would result in him running in circles
around whichever gate we were temporarily at, hugging
strangers' legs, and sipping from untended straws. Pierson and
Larson, long over being entertained by airport snacks and the
dwindling contents of our activity bag, spent their time
wrestling, playing chase, and fighting to the death over a one-
and-a-half-inch Lego figure of the Incredible Hulk. Why I
didn't bring a DVD player along for each boy will remain one

of the great mysteries of the modern world. Had I thought they would have enough mind-numbing images on board the ship? Had I thought that traveling with my kids should be a time of fun and old-fashioned games? Had I been smoking crack when I planned this? Who knows? But it will never happen again.

We finally boarded at seven, then sat on the runway for forty minutes. Somehow the shuffling around had resulted in the four of us being upgraded to first class. The extra leg room was nice, but first-class passengers have a heightened level of expectations and no one wanted to be in the vicinity of two exhausted, whining boys and a toddler with poop in his diaper.

Shortly after takeoff, the exhausted boys all fell asleep, and I was able to enjoy a quiet meal of airplane food, which is exactly the quality of food to which I had grown accustomed. The angelic faces around me were certainly a blessing, at least until they became a curse as I tried to get them all and our luggage from La Guardia to Manhattan at eleven P.M.

However I did it, I was pleased to put them all to bed that night in a mouse-free environment—no origami-animal-shaped towels, no mouse chocolates on the pillows. I still had two days to go until the big boys returned from the dude ranch, but who cared, really? I had survived a vacation with four of my children, and now I never had to do that again. Or at least not until Fox makes a cruise on which Lois and Petah are at the captain's table, seated next to Marge and Homer, and Finn can run wild with the likes of Maggie, Stewie, and Brian. Perhaps I'll send Peter on that cruise with the kids. I will stay here in New York and go on my own safari to bag the big five: Bergdorf's, Bloomingdale's, Barneys, Bendel's, and Saks.

"I grabbed the extinguisher and pointed it at the
coniferno."

HOLIDAZE

LET'S JUST DISPENSE WITH MY LEAST FAVORITE holiday right up front: Christmas. it's not that I am Grinchy, nor am I guilt-ridden over the obvious excess required to celebrate the holiday with six children—I love giving my kids gifts and paving the house with new toys that will be dismissed and forgotten within fifteen minutes of unwrapping. I *love* that. What I can't bear is the escalating expectations and ultimate pressure associated with all things year-end. There is absolutely nothing to buy for these kids; we already own every version of every toy ever made, and even coming up with a decent show underneath the tree has become a hassle. How many Batman figures does Larson really need to own? My older boys are always happy with the latest video game, but that doesn't make much of a pile, and for my little men, it's all about the show. Clothes? Forget it, they'd kill me on the spot. Books. Sure, if you like hearing your kid groan when he opens a package. I tear my hair out trying to come up with big stuff and lots of it. Peter tries to help, but usually comes home with the Radio Shack 200 in 1 Electronics Lab, forgetting we still have the ones he bought the previous three years in the closet.

December is the month when, regardless of how equal a marriage may seem on the outside, mom is left holding Santa's bag, or lighting the candles, whatever her religion requires. I can't bring myself to do the Christmas card thing; I'd have to start thinking of a setting back in August. What will best represent how fantastic we are as parents and how blissfully happy our children are? A sunny beach? A pristine white ski slope? How would I get all of our children decent-looking and smiling in front of a camera? Getting six children to sit still for .2 seconds is not as easy as it seems. Then I'd need to find a stand-in for my daughter, who is never around, and spend hours Photoshopping her face onto the surrogate, not to mention Photoshopping out somebody's pinkeye infection and the bunny ears Peik made behind Truman's head. The entire process is just so exhausting. I have yet to organize a database of addresses, so even if I did have the wherewithal to get a card made, I doubt it would actually be sent out. I have a friend who never sends me a card for Christmas, but instead sends one on Valentine's Day. It's a brilliant idea; not only does she have an extra six weeks of downtime to execute this thankless task, but the card arrives after the chaos of the holidays and I actually have a moment to enjoy it. I am seriously considering Arbor Day cards.

During the countdown to Christmas break, four backpacks enter my home every day, chock-full of announcements of school fund-raisers, recitals, end-of-trimester parent-teacher conferences (why does a preschooler need a conference?), and birthday party invitations ("I hope Truman can make it, it's sooo hard for Christian to have a Christmastime birthday")— a constant stream of paper working its way into my house, bent and creased and greasy and each single piece expressing its claim to a pound of my flesh. And then there are all the "Winter Solstice" events at Larson's international preschool, because God forbid Christmas should take up all of our attention: we also have to find time each December to teach our children to be tolerant of others. Don't even get me started on all the tipping and gifting—of teachers, teachers' aides, teachers' assistants, nannies, mannies, therapists, parking garage attendants, postal delivery facilitators (formerly known as "mailmen"), secret Santas, and class moms. My bank is broken along with my spirit of giving.

How did spreading holiday cheer become women's work? How many men actually make it to a holiday singalong past pre-k? And of the few who do, is it even remotely possible that they have sewn some sequins on Mary's blue headdress or run down to the 99-cent store the morning of the big show, praying that there are three fuzzy Santa hats left?

During this hundred-yard dash to the five-minute finish line of opening presents on Christmas morning, all children lose what shreds of common sense they might have had the month before. They may spend eleven months of the year jockeying for position on my favorite-child list, but come

November 30 they are gaming Santa, even the ones who no longer believe. Like most parents with children hopped up on snowman-shaped cookies and dreams of the latest iPod, Peter and I wield the old fat man like a cudgel. Every other sentence out of my mouth is a shouted "Santa's watching you!" After many repetitions of this threat, I sometimes have to take myself into the bathroom and soak my face in a sink full of ice water to keep from going insane. Who am I? How did I become this harpy, demanding that my children answer to a fictitious red-and-white executioner?

As if all of the above weren't enough, in the middle of the month my children are handed over to me for twenty days of "school break," backpacks now stuffed with "projects" and "homework" to be done during our holiday "downtime." Because, of course, there is nothing a child wants to do more than spend a vacation working. Talk about a busman's holiday. Seriously, can we stop with the break projects? Does my six-year-old really need to make a photo collage all about him? Must my ten-year-old sculpt clay figures of middle grass prairie life? Yes, I know that education is an ongoing process and that without my careful tending they will slowly forget everything they have learned in the past few months, but if you're so worried about them then don't give them to me for twenty straight days. When the nannies and teachers and therapists all disappear on me, I find myself in the dubious position of having to take care of my own kids. I have to walk away from my career and go on sabbatical, completely and without reservation, in order to satisfy all the sugarplum dreams of this pack of wolves. They have been promised so much by the media and by the world at large that I am nearly blinded by the crush of responsibility. They have to be fed, for one thing, and entertained, for another. Why add algebra?

Because of the exorbitant cost of traveling at Christmas, it has become our habit to head for the local "mountain," armed with ski passes bought at a discount during the off-season. One year, I was too pregnant to decamp to the country for the holidays. The more babies you have, the faster they deliver, so my doctor wanted me in town in case the little one decided to pull a baby Jesus on us. We cobbled together some decorations from the 99-cent shop (my Christmastime go-to), and put up a tree in the apartment. The questions about how Santa would get in without a chimney went unanswered, Christmas passed, and for months the tree stood in the corner. Many months. We had found some energy and focus back in February to take off the decorations, but now the bare tree stood there, taking up precious urban square footage. I would like to blame the new-baby tumult, but the truth is that getting rid of a tree in New York City is not an easy feat. The Parks Department will pick them up and make them into environmentally friendly post-holiday mulch, but pickup is only on certain days, and I never seem to get the memo.

In the country, we just drag our tree outside and burn it. This sparked an idea. It occurred to me that I had never used a fire extinguisher and that perhaps it would be good to know how one works—you know, in case of an emergency. So, in the ultimate what-were-you-thinking moment, we gathered around the city tree, Peter included (so I can't be the only adult blamed for this), and someone held a lighter to a dry, crackly branch. It wasn't me, as I was tasked with actually putting the fire out so I was standing by with the extinguisher locked and loaded. I'm a pretty good shot with a rifle; how hard could this be? The moment the first needle caught fire, the entire six-foot tree exploded into flames. Why this result was so unexpected is a mystery to me even now, but it caused me to scream and at the same time completely forget that I was the one assigned with putting the damn thing out. I grabbed the extinguisher and aimed it at the coniferno. It stopped burning as quickly as it had started. As I looked around at the apartment, I realized the true lesson of how fire extinguishers work, and why they should be used only in case of emergency: the entire apartment was covered in a fine white powder, every crack, every crevice, every curlicue of my husband's grandmother's elaborately carved French provincial armoire.

"Ai-ai-ai," Zoila said as she looked upon the scene, shaking her head and no doubt wondering at how we can create a fresh new hell for her at every turn.

Unfortunately, I don't have a Zoila upstate to deal with the magnitude of our collective messes, so during the holidays most of the crime scene investigations are handled by yours truly. As you can imagine, it is a constant job, with armloads of toys to remove from one part of the house to the next, and countless hours spent washing clothes, dishes, and weenies. The kids do seem to have a good time, but there are a few fundamental problems for me. First and foremost, I am a warm-weather gal, and I fear the cold the way some people fear man smell, or taxes. Temperatures in the below-zeros are common-place in the Berkshires. I don't care if my children get frost-bite—they can still grow new toes—but me? There is only so much time a woman with my taste in shoes can spend wearing Uggly boots, and at about an hour I pass my limit. The occasional stroll out to the pond on a weekend is one thing; hanging out on a snow-covered mountain all afternoon quite another.

These ski vacations hold little interest for me because I don't ski. I don't understand the appeal of a sport that often results in tearing something that makes your knee stop work ing. Best-case scenario, I am careening down a mountain at high speed, out of control. Worst case, I am on my ass, cold and wet. And why would I willingly engage in a sport that requires me to wear puffy clothes that make me look fat? I much prefer the cute white pleated skirts suitable for summer sports, or the regal gear worn for riding. Naturally, because I can't leave the house for fear of the cold and hideous footwear, I am stuck cooking and cleaning, two activities I also try to avoid. I do feel a responsibility to put in equal time—Peter gets the boys to the mountain every cold morning, so the least I can do is have something warm waiting for them to eat, even if that means throwing something from the bottom of the freezer in the oven.

As much as I love my husband, once the novelty of skiing with his children wears off he reverts to wandering around inside, looking for something to "fix." I find myself wondering around day ten of Christmas break whether he has any errands that will get him out of my hair. I think he must feel the need to get away from me, also, because he starts to focus on minutiae that he otherwise tends to overlook.

"Look at the bottom of these pots," he says a day after New Year's. Yes, I actually tried to cook real food for New Year's Day, and these are the thanks I get.

"Okay," I say, not looking up from my computer, where I'm trying to sneak in a little work so I'm not swallowed up the following week.

"These are expensive pots," he continues. "If you don't scrub the bottoms, this gunk will get cooked on and become impossible to remove."

"Peter, are all the children alive and accounted for?" I ask, glancing up at him.

"Well, yes," he says, still holding the offending pot bottom up.

"I think we need milk. And see if you can't run past Big Y and pick up some pot scrubbers while you're out."

"I'll be right back," he says, conceding the point. Our condition can only be accurately described as too much togetherness, or overwhelming Christmas spirit.

When Peter returns a couple of hours later, he's brought me a surprise, entering the house loaded down with Kmart bags.

"Now, that's what I'm talking about!" I say, taking the bags from him and peeking inside. We have an annual tradition of buying up all the reduced-price gaudy ornaments that Kmart has to offer.

"Look at these." Peter pulls a box of large round red ones with flocked snowmen on them.

"Fantastic," I say. "Let's hang them up!"

He grabs a couple more boxes and walks out the kitchen door, while I race down the hall to the gun cabinet to retrieve my personal favorite, a high-powered German pellet rifle, and a box of ammo. I run back into the kitchen and open the window over the sink. By the time I get my rifle loaded, Peter has hung about twenty odd-size ornaments fifty yards away on a nail-studded plank designed for this purpose.

"All clear!" he yells, running back to the house to join me. I can't tell you how many houseguests have enjoyed this activity. Even the kids get into the action with assorted BB guns. Before you know it, every window on the north side of the house is open and tiny Santas and reindeer are being blown to smithereens. When the last one has been dispatched, Peter turns to me, my very own Mr. Smith & Wesson, gun still slightly smoking.

"Good work keeping the kids alive," he says, and gives me a high-five.

Just barely alive. Little did he know that while he was out, the four elder boys went a little stir crazy; in their moment of severe cabin fever, they decided to collect all the cardboard boxes from the various presents and construct a giant fort in the kitchen. I was getting Finn up from his nap when I heard yelling from downstairs.

"Fire in the hole!" Pierson shouted, and though I know he is prone to drama, I raced back down, a half-naked Finn on my hip. Smoke curled out of the kitchen and I got there just in time to see Peik throwing water on a black chunk of cardboard and Truman slapping the same area with a wet dishtowel. Pierson stood in the corner, fire extinguisher sort of at the ready. Though, like his mother before him, he didn't have the sense to actually point and shoot.

"Who set this on fire?" I demanded. They all just stood there, a *tableau de Noël*.

"It wasn't me!" cried Pierson.

"Spontaneous combustion?" Peik managed. They all looked at him, nodding in agreement, and then looked back at me, praying for believability.

"I have read *Ripley's Believe It or Not,*" I said, looking each of them dead in the eye. "And I know for certain that spontaneous combustion only happens in obscure English villages. You're all guilty, but I'm going to turn my back and the ringleader can put his matches on the table." When I turned around there was a box for each boy. Perhaps I should have tried to teach them something while I had them, after all. Like, "Let your brother take the fall," or "Don't play with matches." I really felt sorry for them in that moment. What they really needed was to be back in school. Fast. By the time the holidays were officially over, every last one of us was happy to see the last of the others.

SINCE I MOVED TO THE NORTHEAST, I'M NOT REALLY THAT INTO Easter. I generally try to avoid it altogether. In my opinion, Easter should look very springy, and when the temperature is thirty-seven degrees and my kids are running around in fleece instead of pristine white embroidered short sets, it just doesn't feel right. My kids know that they have a day off from school, but they don't seem completely clear on the difference between Easter and Passover, though they're aware that we aren't Jewish. I can usually avoid having to fill baskets on Easter by just not mentioning that it is Easter Sunday. This only works if I can prevent the kids from noticing that *It's the Easter Beagle, Charlie Brown* is on and if I can keep them away from the Peeps display at Rite Aid. Otherwise, I'm busted and have to search the basement for baskets and scrounge the kitchen for candy.

Halloween is the big holiday in our family. It's the perfect example of how a low-expectation event can blow away the most jaded partygoer if you put in extra effort and preparation. We have amassed a cache of Hollywood-prop-room-worthy decorations and begin putting them up around October 1. Enter our loft on any day thereafter, and you are likely to find me on a ladder, hand-sewing formations of life-size rubber bats to the sprinkler pipes that run along the ceiling, or strategically placing rotting rubber corpses.

For some reason, my boys have no interest in my design talents and want to wear store-bought costumes, but my own is carefully crafted. I wear an iteration of the same theme every year: the mad scientist's creature. One look at Peter should tell you who plays the mad scientist. All we need to do for him is throw a lab coat over whatever he happens to be wearing on October 31, tease his locks up a little bit higher, and voilà! The execution of my getup is slightly more complicated, as it requires three main components: an elaborate wig, a latex dress, and a pair of freaky white contacts.

I care so deeply about this particular holiday that a few years ago I had myself fitted for top-grade, straight-out-of-a-horror-movie zombie eyes. These lenses white out my irises completely, except for a small black spot in the center to see through. Their design is very clever—imagine a white doughnut painted on a contact lens—and the effect is ultra creepy. I can see perfectly with them in, and they are comfortable, but I have one problem: I cannot get them either in or out by myself. For all the gory and disgusting things I can put up with around me for this occasion—the fake blood, the bowl of "intestines," and so on—I am grossed out to the point of fainting by the idea of my finger making contact with my eye. This year I went upstairs to my neighbor's apartment and she slipped them in, amid much blinking and tearing, but clearly I couldn't go see her at one A.M. to ask her to take them out. I slept in them and tried to get them out by myself the next morning, to no avail. Peter is equally as eyeball averse as I am, so I needed to find someone less squeamish.

"Mom, really, I'll make my own breakfast," Truman said as he bumped into me in the kitchen. "I can't look at you."

"Truman, do Mommy a favor and help her get these things out?" I pleaded. "I have a meeting in an hour, and I can't show up like this." I rolled my eyes for effect. He backed away, forgoing food and practically running for the door.

I would have asked his older brother, but one look at Peik's nails after a night of partying suggested otherwise. I finally tracked down Peter. Not only had I run out of boys, but also, I figured they'd had enough of me and my costume needs after the annual get-Mom-into-her-latex-dress event the afternoon before.

Many people have a favorite Thanksgiving dish; for me it wouldn't be Halloween without latex. My dress this year was black, knee length, and backless, with long sleeves and buckles at the neck and waist. I bought it at a fetish shop in the East Village, one of the last New York neighborhoods that hasn't been sanitized of its sex shops.

Wearing latex is quite ritualistic, and latex garments are difficult to get into. First, you cover your body with baby powder, sprinkling the inside of the garment as well. Then you step into the dress and sort of roll it up—hoping to align it properly, because it is nearly impossible to reposition once on. Once you're dressed, there is baby powder everywhere and polishing to be done. The boys, each equipped with a handful of silicone gel, rub me down until I shine like a brand-new sex toy in a Times Square window (before Disney, that is). I can only wonder what lasting effects this activity will have on their sexuality, but I figure they will end up in therapy for some reason, so why not make life interesting for their eventual shrinks? You spend that kind of money, someone better be entertained.

Halloween starts about an hour after I don the giant albino Afro wig and six-inch Jimmy Choos. I now clear seven feet easily. As long as I don't drink, I won't need to pee. Mayhem breaks out at about five, when packs of kids large to small arrive. The undead fill our loft to the rafters, and even those who dare to show up without costumes take on an eerie glow in the strobe lights and artificial fog. Kids eat way too much candy, and adults drink way too much liquor, as evidenced by the inevitable "Thriller" dance performed by the entire crowd.

This year Peter and I broke free around nine, leaving the kick-out and cleanup to Nicole and Alicia, much stricter and more capable enforcers than we'll ever be. I was quite excited to be invited to a fancy party to benefit Central Park. I have to say my husband and I really stood out in a sea of Sarah Palins: Sarah and John, Sarah and Bristol, Sarah and Moose, Sarah as beauty queen, and countless pigs in lipstick. I had carefully placed a top hat on my 'fro, making me pretty much the tallest dominatrix in the place, as well as the shiniest. Peter led me around the venue, in all my fabulousness, and still the only comment I heard repeatedly was "Do you think that's his real hair?"

THE ONLY OTHER HOLIDAY WE CELEBRATE ON ANY REGULAR BASIS IS Thanksgiving. After our full-on approach to Halloween, and before the oppressive approach of Christmas, I choose to get as far under the turkey radar as possible. Thanksgiving is supposed to be about giving thanks, but everyone knows it is really about food. As you probably know by now, I hate cooking and am not especially fond of eating, so I've found a way around slaving over a meal that no one in my family is particularly interested in. Luckily, here in the city we have an amazing grocery-delivery service called Fresh Direct. My family would starve without this modern convenience: with just a few magical clicks of my mouse, I order a meal to my specifications, and the very next day Delivery Dude shows up at my door with a fully cooked Thanksgiving dinner, complete with side dishes and zucchini bread. They even send along a little meat thermometer in case you're feeling guilty and want to overinvolve yourself in the reheating of the fully cooked bird. Years ago, Cleo was horrified when she arrived home from boarding school to find our first feast-in-a-box; she announced that even though the Thanksgivings up to that point had been inedible, this was just "wrong." Her longing for June Cleaver has finally subsided, or maybe she has given up, and now the arrival of the Dude is not only a given, but a time-honored family tradition.

WE DID TRY AND ENGAGE THE HOLIDAY IN A REAL WAY ONCE. WE live three blocks away from Macy's, but usually don't go to the big parade—as soon as we moved into the neighborhood, we discovered it is basically a made-for-television event, with camera trucks completely corralling the store itself and for twenty blocks up Broadway. Only if you're well connected can you get the premium bleacher seating, but even for that you have to be there a good two hours before the parade even starts, and Thanksgiving is typically the nastiest, coldest day on the planet. What child will sit still, packed in amid total strangers, for three hours waiting for a giant Clifford to float overhead, when he can watch the same thing in the warmth of his own home mere minutes away? That having been asked, one year Peter summoned his courage and took four of the boys to see the various acts practice the night before the actual event. I was unpacking dinner for the next day and also obesely pregnant with Finn, so Peter dared this outing alone, depending on the slightly older boys to help keep track of the much younger ones. Larson, three years old, highly speech impaired, and lightning fast, waited for Peter to turn his head and slipped away. Panic ensued, with Peik stopping every police officer he could find, Truman shouting Larson's name over the blasting loudspeakers, and Pierson just plain freaking out, which is a mystery to me because he never seemed to care much about the child before he was lost.

"Which superhero was he wearing?" Peter yelled at Pierson, holding him by the shoulders while clutches of families squeezed by, using this moment of confusion to slip in front of the Shelton pack for a better view.

"I . . . don't . . . know!" Pierson sobbed.

"Think!" Peter commanded. "Was it Spider-Man or Superman?!"

"Spider-Man on top, Superman on the bottom!" Pierson finally managed, relieved to have contributed in some way.

"Dad, look!" Truman shouted from the top of the bleachers, pointing toward the middle of the performance area. Peter, Peik, and Pierson all scrambled up to see Larson, in the middle of a clutch of majorettes, surrounded by a giant marching band pumping out a brassy version of "We Are Family," having the time of his little unintelligible life. One of the cops waded into the swirling instruments and pompoms, picked him up, and hoisted him onto his shoulders as the crowd went wild.

Acknowledgments

■ ■ ■ ■ ■ ■ ■ ■ ■ ■ ■ ■ ■

SOMETIMES IT IS HARD TO REMEMBER THAT THANKSGIVING IS ABOUT giving thanks. I do not believe in God, exactly, but I do believe in some kind of universal cosmic force, and to this force, I would like to take a moment to mention the things I am most thankful for. Though, being all-powerful, it probably already knows.

I am thankful for Fresh Direct, as it saves me from having to shop for food at Duane Reade Pharmacy, which is a very good thing because you can only serve Frosted Flakes and ramen noodles for dinner so many times before one of your kids calls Child Protective Services. I am also thankful for paper plates, because I detest not only shopping and cooking but also the aftermath. Cleanup is exponentially easier when I can just plow the leavings of the dinner table into the garbage can.

I am thankful for Adderall, Ritalin, Focalin, et cetera, because a medicated child is a happy child. Likewise, I am thankful for Nicorette gum, Dunkin' Donuts coffee, and Tanqueray martinis straight up with olives, because a medicated parent is a happy parent.

I am thankful for my personal technology, whose artificial intelligence surpasses my own. Spell-check: you are brilliant, and if not for you this book would read as if Larson had written it. To iPod shuffle: playing "Stairway to Heaven" and "Highway to Hell" back to back was a stroke of genius. If there is a god, you are probably it.

I am thankful for my long-wear lipstick and my power panties. You keep my lips and ass in place, respectively, and save me valuable time in front of mirrors. And my beloved Birkin bag, not only do you faithfully carry around all the crap required to get me through my day, but you offer me a sense of security: if I ever decide to split this scene, I can stop by that high-end resale shop on Eighteenth Street on my way out of town and raise enough cash on you and your little sister to live for six months. Throw in Judith Leiber and I get a whole year!

I am thankful for my girls, Alicia and Nicole. Your hard work and dedication keep me from becoming a homicidal bitch. And Zoila, my husband's true wife: other women in his life have come and gone, but for thirty years, you have been there for him, and you've never once washed his cell phone. Sorry again, Peter. I am equally thankful for Blake, our manny, because only a gay man would have found the show tunes channel on XM and served it with breakfast.

I am thankful for my family. For Peter, who never complains about the price of my Manolos, though his accountant hates the fact that I charge them to his business American Express and has repeatedly asked me to stop. Peter has never asked me to stop, and until I get the word from the big guy, I'm taking that as a "You just go ahead, honey." I am thankful for my hilarious kids, who are a constant source of good writing material. Believe me, I couldn't make this stuff up. I am thankful that my daughter attends a state college—wow, what a tuition break. I am thankful that my father taught me to shoot, and my mother taught me to sew, because being a size 6 on the top and size 8 on the bottom makes it impossible to buy a dress off the rack.

And finally, I am thankful that my in-laws are dead, because I can serve Thanksgiving dinner out of a box and straight onto paper plates without feeling like a failure.

Acknowledgments

BELIEVE IT OR NOT, I HAVE MORE THANKS TO GIVE.

First and foremost I want to give a special shout-out to the brilliant Amy Scheibe. Her contributions as editor and co-writer were invaluable. I would never have been able to structure this book without her hilarious moments, unending patience, phenomenal organizational skills, and lattes. She truly helped me sew a pile of mismatched patches into a cohesive, well-constructed garment.

I would also like to thank Benjamin Dreyer for dreaming up the entire scheme and lining up the players. Susan Mercandetti, I know it's cheesy to claim that a writer has become friends with her editor, but in this case it is true, at least until I try to sell her another book. Ben Steinberg, for stepping in when I was in full panic mode and talking me down off the ledge. Robert Best for the illustrations, because every girl wants to look like Barbie.

LAURA BENNETT wowed viewers of *Project Runway's* season 3 with her jaw-dropping outspokenness and sophisticated designs. She has a large and growing fan base thanks to *Project Runway,* MSN's "Glam Squad" StyleStudio, and QVC, which sells her designs. Bennett writes the *Case Clothed* comic strip for iVillage and a column for The Daily Beast. She lives in Manhattan.

www.didntifeedyouyesterday.com

ABOUT THE TYPE

This book was set in Garamond, a typeface designed by the French printer Jean Jannon. It is styled after Garamond's original models. The face is dignified, and is light but without fragile lines. The italic is modeled after a font of Granjon, which was probably cut in the middle of the sixteenth century.